My Three Lives

An Adventure in Living

To Elayne:
thanks for your friendship!
Cavell

Cavell Butt Tyrrell

tellwell

Tellwell Talent
www.tellwell.ca

ISBN
978-0-2288-2316-2 (Paperback)

DEDICATION

To my sons Paul, Christopher and Edward that they may better know their mother's roots and their own.

To my dear husband, Len, who gave me the space to be myself and grow. Thank you "sweet man."

To my parents who left much too early but gave my sisters and me a solid grounding and love of life. You did it!

TABLE OF CONTENTS

ACKNOWLEDGEMENTS

MARGARET WHITTAKER, whose expertise helped this story through its growing pains.

MATTHEW KLEINOSKY, who kept my computer and me on friendly terms.

SANDRA LEWIS, author and my canoeing partner for her enthusiasm and encouragement.

PAUL, CHRISTOPHER AND EDWARD, my sons, for their support and encouragement. Without you my life would be much the poorer. Thank you for joining this family!

DARIN STEINKEY, my long suffering editor who has helped make this story so much more readable.

RHEA MAE for helping me all throughout the publication process of my book.

Cavell Butt Tyrrell, born in the Dominion of Newfoundland in 1927.

Landed immigrant to Dominion of Canada in 1942.

Registered nurse, World War II veteran, historian, voyageur, adventurer.

At 92, living out the extended phase of her life among her wonderful friends at Christie Gardens, the Toronto retirement community with the "mostest."

FOREWORD

In the year 2000, at the request of my youngest sister, Shirley, then in her sixty-fifth year, I began to write our family story. Shirley was only two years old when our father died, and she had no memory of us as a family, so she felt this empty space in her memory keenly. All I intended to write about was the St. George's part of our story, which included the early part of Shirley's childhood. As the years went by, however, the questions from my growing sons encouraged me to complete the story, which now spans almost 100 years from 1927 to 2020.

I also came to feel that I would like to do it for my own sake. I thought to look at my life, its chapters, and the experiences that shaped the person I am would be useful for my inner growth.

I always knew I needed to begin this story in Newfoundland and now, in 2000, I'm finally in St. George's on the west coast of Newfoundland where my sisters and I were born. I've found a place out of the wind and from here I can look out over the harbour across to Sandy Point and beyond the wide stretch of water to Stephenville.

This low flying cloudy sky, the big whitecaps and the dark water bring up a feeling of home. It's the wind and sea that remind me of my childhood. On days like this in Toronto or Temagami, Ontario, where we canoe, when the wind is blowing, the sky is blue and the clouds are moving fast, I say to myself or to whoever is around, "This is a St. George's day." I love the wind wherever I am and today, in St. George's looking out to sea, I am back where I first knew it!

From where I'm sitting in the protection of a high bank, I can look out to the spot where we sprinkled the ashes of my sister, Phyllis, three years ago. At her request we brought her home from California to the place she loved so well.

The pink sandy beach where we played as children and learned to swim; the big white house set back from the sea; the cemetery up the road where our father is buried along with his parents and grandparents—my forbearers—all this is home to me. Toronto is where I live but the basic feeling of home is here. It's almost as though St. George's is set in my bones.

Perhaps human beings are wired like that; perhaps there's a part of us that's set in place by the geography and the energy of the place where we are born. It is against this feeling that we measure all the other places we may live. Though we may feel at home elsewhere, there's something that clicks when we return to our original land.

At least, it's that way for me.

I was aware of a great contentment yesterday as the boat from Nova Scotia neared Port aux Basques and Newfoundland. As we drove along the countryside, I felt an empty spot being filled in. I've wondered if this feeling is even more pronounced in people who have had to leave their homes in their formative years. I was nine when I left, and I missed it more than I could express at the time.

I missed the big grassy meadow filled with buttercups and daisies. I missed the big old house where there were so many rooms to explore. I missed our cow, Daisy—she felt like a part of the family for we had no pets. I missed my cousin, Audrey, my friend and playmate, even more than May and Mary Pieroway who were also our playmates. And I especially missed the sea, which had been part of my everyday. I couldn't go to the barn, the woodshed, the vegetable garden or the henhouse without being aware of it; the sea was part of my very being.

Living in St. George's as a child seems eons ago in one way but as I sit here looking at the familiar landscape, I'm still that little girl running through the grass, climbing the fence and running down the bank to the water. I'm in my bare feet and there is a wind blowing, the sun is shining, and I feel wonderful. If it is after supper and the sun is beginning to set, the sky is lit up with the most wonderful shades of rose, purple, apricot and aquamarine. It opens my heart and I feel a oneness with all that is.

I've come to realize this book will be a collection of childhood memories that left an impression on me as they occurred and are not necessarily chronological. As one memory brings up another, it's as though I'm reliving the experience. It's a good feeling!

Part 1

ST. GEORGE'S, NEWFOUNDLAND, 1927-1937

My First Home

BEGINNINGS

I was born on the first day of summer, June 21, 1927, in a house by the sea in St. George's, Newfoundland. My grandfather, Captain Nathaniel Butt, a sea captain who made his living trading between Newfoundland and the eastern seaboard of North America built the house for his growing family. He chose "neoclassical" architecture, as was the style being built at the time in Canada and the United States. My father, Samuel, was the first child born in it on August 15, 1882.

To my young eyes the house felt like a solid, secure island in a sea of grass and wildflowers. The corner trim and the windows with their moulded decorative brackets sported a deep green as they looked out over the harbour to Sandy Point and beyond to Cape St. George.

I was a Tuesday baby and at nine pounds was the first of three daughters born to Samuel Butt and Mary Norman. At forty-five, my father must have been delighted to be starting his family. He really enjoyed his children. Family snapshots show him holding me as a young baby. In another, he is lying on the grass giving me a steadying hand as I was standing alone, almost, on my first birthday. He looks contented and proud in all of them.

I was born when my mother was twenty-five and had been married less than a year. I'm sure it was a great relief to her that I waited the extra day after their nine-month wedding anniversary. THAT MATTERED in our society at the time! Phyllis came along two years after me and was my closest playmate for years as there were no other children nearby.

I was named after my mother's only sister, Bessie Vardy, and father's sister, Ruth Morris, just so things were fair—no favourites! The name Cavell was mine alone. I was named after Edith Cavell, a British World War I nurse who was executed by the German forces of occupation in Belgium. She, a civilian matron of a Brussels hospital, was tried by a military court for allegedly helping British soldiers escape. She was shot at dawn the next morning. The British soldiers' sense of chivalry toward women was outraged as was the world's. My father, in the Royal Newfoundland Regiment, was a soldier in France at the time and ten years later my name was waiting for me!

My world stretched in four directions to the fences, and that was all right with me; there was lots of room. The fences never felt confining. They were friendly. They connected us to our relatives: Norman Butt, Dad's first cousin on one side; George Pieroway, Dad's first cousin on his mother's side on the other. Beyond him was George's father, Uncle Johnnie, Grandma Butt's brother. Behind us were Dad's brother, Uncle Alfred, and another brother, Uncle Hilliard. We were surrounded by family.

On the other side of the fence, the sea seemed to have a life of its own. It moved with the wind and set the dories and motor boats dancing jigs out on their boat collar. These anchorages were in deeper water where the tides would not leave the boats high and dry. Across the water was Sandy Point, a busy port with the boats coming and going all day. At night, the oil lamps from the dozens of homes were warm and friendly. On stormy days when the rain came down in slanting sheets, the boats leaped about, the sea and sky were grey, and the wind howled about the house. On sunny days, which was most of the time once summer settled in, the wind blew softly but purposefully from the west. Isn't there a Masefield poem that speaks of the sea and the wind? When I read the poem years later it was our field and meadow that I saw with Mom at the clothesline, her skirt flapping around her legs.

Our field was a wonderful place to play. Wild roses grew on Norman Butt's fence in the summer. In the fall, the flowers turned to rosehips, which one year Phyllis and I strung into a necklace. Unfortunately, so we felt, our mother became so enthused that we found ourselves stringing long ropes of these orangey-red hips to adorn the Harvest Home arrangement at the front of the church on Thanksgiving Sunday! Our fun had turned into work, but they did look wonderful up there, and our mother was very proud of her daughters!

My favourite fence was the one that ran along the bank. The "longers," polished grey from the sun, wind and rain, made a perfect ladder. Once my head and shoulders cleared the topmost rail my world opened like magic! On my right, I saw "the factory," my dad's facility next to the big government wharf where he canned lobster and salmon in season. On my left I saw the tops of "red rocks" where the water was deep and where the big kids were allowed to swim.

TSUNAMI/TIDAL WAVE

In the autumn of 1929, a devastating tidal wave caused untold damage and hardship in Newfoundland. As far as I know, we had no warning. Nobody we knew had radios or even telephones and the water seeped in with surprising speed. If there had been warning there wouldn't have been such losses. People in St. George's didn't know about it until the water started to rise. It covered the wide beach first, then the fishermen's storage buildings began to sway as it climbed the bank. Dad was somewhere between our place and the factory helping where he could, and Mom was on her own with Phyllis and me. I can't believe a child can remember events at just over two years of age, but I can. Perhaps being so scared helped. No doubt some of the details come from people's retelling through the years, but I have several vivid memories of that day.

I remember seeing the harbour full of red water and that was strange. Our water wasn't that colour! I can still see boats floating by on the red water with nobody in them. I knew that was serious because someone was losing their boat! Uncle Alfred's fishing store at the bottom of the bank below our house was rocking in the water and that was scary. If that building could rock, would our house start to do that too? Probably the most worrisome aspect for me was the water rising up the red sandstone bank.

Even at that age I knew deep water was dangerous and here it was coming up to where we were. I was sure it would get us! Mom assured me that it wouldn't come up that far, but I still wanted to check it out every few minutes. I wasn't allowed to go down to the bank by myself for I imagine Mom could see me investigating to the point of danger, so I had to wait for her. We went frequently. I had to hold her hand and five-month-old Phyllis was on her arm.

We all wished Dad would come home so we could know that he was all right, but he didn't arrive for a long time. When he did, it was only then that we heard the full extent of the damage in St. George's. All the fishing stores except for one or two were gone along with their wharves and many boats. There had been no time to secure them nor anywhere for them to go. The stores not only held the fishermen's nets and supplies but a good part of the current year's harvest of dried fish, their only source of income. Nobody had insurance; that was something new and in any case was unaffordable.

The damage on our west coast was considerable but on the south coast, which was in a direct line with the underwater earthquake, the government help was only for the hardest hit and then it was only a pittance. Some people there lost their homes as well as their food for the winter. Many lost their lives. That tidal wave is burned in the memories of many people.

Most of the fishing stores on the beach in St. George's were not rebuilt and the beach still carries the scars. The stumps of some of the foundations are still there along with the piles of rocks that formed the foundations of the small wharves.

We later learned that our father had jumped from someone's wharf into a boat floating by in order to save it. He didn't know whose boat it was but that was beside the point to Dad. He knew somebody needed that boat and he could help.

MY BAREFOOT SUMMER

Summer really began in earnest when I was allowed to go barefoot. I began pestering Mom long before it was warm enough and—for what seemed an eternity—the answer was always "no." Then one sunny day the answer was "yes!" and I felt like I would burst as I ripped off my shoes and socks. I was free of that layer of leather that separated me from the earth! Underfoot, the grass felt cool and damp but cushiony and friendly. I loved it and my world expanded!

When we were old enough, around five or six, we were allowed to play on the beach as long as we asked before we climbed the fence, scampered across the few feet of grass on the bank and dropped to the beach below. Down there, out of sight of the house, we were trusted not to put our feet in the water unless we first checked with Mom. I now know this was her safety strategy but at the time it was such a pain!

It was August before we could walk around in the water to "paddle" and then go no deeper than our knees. But at last we could finally get at the interesting stuff that had been out of reach: coloured stones and glass that had been rounded and polished by the sea, and the long banners of kelp and seaweed that had bladders the size of grapes that went "pop!" when we squeezed them even though the adults said they would give us warts! Where the old wharves had been before the tidal wave there were piles of rocks covered with blue mussels that we would take back to the house to cook up for a treat and look for pearls. Occasionally we found a few pearls and there would be great whoops of delight, but these were soon lost as they were so small. Stanley Grimshaw, my cousin from Toronto who spent his summers with Aunt Mary, his grandmother, ate them raw, much to our disgust!

By August when the occasional iceberg that had escaped the cold Labrador current had made its way down Newfoundland's west coast melted or moved on, the water warmed up a bit and we were allowed to go swimming! This was the earliest we could swim and only on a hot day. "Hot" was 70F or 20C and then people complained of the heat! A few of the children swam but none of the adults. My father said he didn't learn to swim because it would only prolong the agony if he fell in. This was the prevailing outlook among these men who lived on the sea. Personal life jackets were unknown.

Once as a young man, Dad fell overboard out on the boat collar, sank to the bottom, oriented himself to the sun and walked ashore, holding his breath. His sister, Mary, who saw him fall in was desperately trying to get a boat out when his head appeared above water twenty or thirty feet from where he fell in!

Mom had an embroidered bathing suit that she made herself. In fact, she made bathing suits for all of us that year. They were made from a blue cotton jersey knit type material. Phyllis and I didn't mind getting them wet, but Dad refused to wear his, let alone get it wet! It would have been like a wet T-shirt contest and he would have nothing to do with it! Right after Mom made them, all of us but Dad wore them at a picnic we had down on the bank. Mom's had a huge embroidered yellow water lily on one hip but I never saw her wear it again. In fact, I never saw her swim.

I think it was around this time that Mom introduced the idea of taking holidays, which she said people were beginning to do. We knew of nobody doing that. People had to be around to accommodate the cycles of the seasons, the animals and the fish. I think Mom was trying to introduce something lighter into our lives.

We had a wonderful water toy that was the envy of our friends, and Phyllis and I used to share it around. After a storm, Dad found a life preserver, a huge white cork thing with the name of the ship painted on the side. I think it eased our parents' minds knowing we had this to help us in the water and we had fun with it, lying across or in it and paddling with our hands. One day when Phyllis was lying through it, instead of flipping back as it usually did, the preserver flipped the other way and Phyllis was trapped head down and feet up. I don't know how long she was like that because there were five or six kids splashing around. Suddenly I saw what was happening and rushed through the waist deep water to tip her up. She was full of water and almost gone. We had to help her stand up and all the way to the shore she coughed and brought up water. We helped her up the bank to the barn where she lay in the hay for a long time until she recovered. We didn't tell Mom until years later for we were sure if we did we would lose the life preserver. We knew we were lucky and had learned what not to do!

One hot day I was splashing around with our friends and pretending to swim (but keeping one foot on the bottom) when someone urged me to take my foot off the bottom and keep my arms and legs moving. Almost instantly I realized I WAS MOVING—I was swimming! The next day Mom came down to Uncle Hilliard's wharf and observed my tremendous accomplishment. I was so proud! Later when I found myself at a huge school in Toronto, no longer the big fish in a small pool and having to work like crazy for average grades, swimming was where I shone and could feel good about myself. I joined the ornamental swim group. I also completed all my Royal Life Saving medals including the real prize, Silver.

OUR OUTDOOR LIFE

On the east side of the field was a lane, a right of way that ran down from the "highroad" to the bank. To get over the fence and into the lane we used the stile, which was a series of steps up one side and down the other. If I climbed to the top step, the view lengthened by quite a bit. One day when I was perched up there, I saw two little girls the same age as Phyllis and me next door in their field! What a discovery! Soon they were at their side of the lane and a friendship had begun! However, for whatever reason our mothers "weren't speaking" so our friendship blossomed in no man's land—the lane!

May and Mary Pieroway become our fast friends and we played together whenever we were outside. We invented our own games and played for hours on end. Years later when I became interested in genealogy, I discovered that May and Mary Pieroway were second cousins!

One memorable game was carrying each other by our arms and legs. There being only four of us meant that one person had to carry both legs or in some cases one leg dragged. Unfortunately for Phyllis one day, I—being in charge of the legs and Phyllis being fairly hefty—found my grip giving way just as we were running over a fresh, wet cow paddy. Phyllis hit the ground and scored a bullseye! Needless to say, Phyllis thought it was deliberate. I got a piece of her mind but we soon patched it up so we could present a united front when we went home to face Mom with manure on her clothes.

Phyllis and I invented another game that involved manure, much to our mother's disapproval! Down in the barn next to the cow's stall was fresh manure from overnight. Outside, through the hole cut in the barn wall, was a pile of manure a couple of feet high where Phyllis took up her position. I was on the inside and had access to the fresh stuff and for a few minutes we tried to throw manure though the hole hoping to be the one to score first! Gradually our aim improved, and I was the first to score, which ended the game when Phyllis went screaming to the house. Our poor mother must have been speechless as Phyllis was wearing her new orange sweater that Mom had just finished knitting!

THE TRAIN

Going down to see the train come in was a big deal. The big black engine puffed into the station where the crew pulled down the big pipe that hung from the big wooden tank holding water for the steam engine. There was a lot of hissing while people alighted from or climbed into the passenger cars, and once the baggage was taken care of, the locomotive got under way. The track was on a bit of a grade and the train took a while to get up to speed but by the time it was passing our field it was doing better and let out a piercing whistle as it neared the level crossing.

I remember being afraid of the train's loud noise and running crying into the house whenever the train was passing our field letting out its ear-splitting warning as it approached the level crossing. Mother's solution was to come outside with me and help me count the cars. I was just learning to count so it turned into a manageable challenge! And I remain a compulsive counter to this day!

One time Phyllis and I were coming home from Arnold Morris' store with some grocery item for Mom when we heard the train approaching from behind. It was on a slight downward slope toward the station and had no trouble with speed coming from the west. It was travelling at a good clip. Because we knew the train often pulled a long string of cars, we realized we would have to wait a while. After some indecision I decided to cross the track. It was coming faster than I realized and even worse, Phyllis, not wanting to be left alone on the other side darted across behind me! Floss Butt was watching from her kitchen window and fully expected to see Phyllis lying dead beside the tracks when the train had passed! She reported the event to Mom, and we were definitely in trouble although I can't remember any consequences.

MY FATHER AS "DAD"

As I mentioned, having a child was a great joy to Dad. He married at forty-four and I was born the following year. There is a picture of him holding me as a baby and his face was happy and tender. He loved having me around and I trailed him everywhere. My earliest memory of my father is of holding his hand as we went off to fix or build something, or just watching while he worked. I never had the feeling that I was in the way. He gave me the great gift of feeling that my contributions were important and though he never said anything about loving me, I knew.

As a soldier in Europe during the First World War and in the Canadian west during the early days of the Depression, he had seen and done a lot and was ready to settle down. He met my mother in St. John's at the home of her sister, Bessie, who was married to his army friend, Jim Vardy. The engagement was short, and they were married in St. George's on September 20, 1926, on her sister's anniversary.

My mom was the only mother I knew who had an engagement ring. I remember asking about it and her telling me that it was a diamond and what it signified. It must have meant a lot to both of them as my dad was not well off, but he was a man of his time, had travelled widely, and I'm sure it meant a lot to him to give it to her.

I later learned that Mother's family didn't approve of the marriage mainly because of the age difference. Dad was forty-four and Mother was twenty-four.

They got along very well for I can remember only twice that I heard an argument. I think they were very much in love because after he died, Mother told me that they always went to sleep at night with her lying in the crook of Dad's arm. My Aunt Bessie, many years later, told me she and Grandma had said to her, "Mary, my dear, you are marrying an older man and someday you will be left with a family of young children." They were right. She was a widow at thirty-five with three children, aged two to nine.

I always watched for Dad coming home for dinner at noon and ran to meet him at the gate. He held my hand and I was content. The road ran along the bank high above the water, and though other men came along from time to time, I learned to recognize my father by his walk. His was a brisk step with a bit of a hop as he compensated for a deep war wound to his back. He never complained. I believe he felt quite grateful to be there considering what he had seen and suffered.

We always had dinner at twelve o'clock and immediately afterward he would lay down on the kitchen couch he had built and sleep for a half hour before going back to work. Though there was lots going on while my mother washed dishes and Phyllis, Shirley and I played, he was able to sleep—probably a legacy from his experiences as a soldier.

As was customary at that time, women did the inside work and men the heavy, cold, dangerous work outside. He didn't seem to need an alarm clock, always getting up when the time came. Even when getting up at three or four o'clock in the morning to go out around the coast collecting lobsters, he didn't need to be wakened.

I spent a lot of time on his knee even when I was school aged. Our newspapers were weekly ones, the *Western Star* from Corner Brook and the *Family Herald* from Montreal. Before I could read, I would perch on his lap looking at the pictures while he read to me. There was a children's column that had interesting stories, and once I had learned to read, he invented a game that we would play. We would read out loud together then suddenly he would cover the story with his hand and both of us would continue reading from memory. I got to be pretty good at reading ahead and it was an exciting game as I got closer to beating him.

He wanted his girls to do well in school. Before I started school he hung a big poster of the alphabet in the corner of the kitchen close to the window for me to memorize. The letters were big, and I can still see their many colours. I practiced often, but it seemed to come so slowly! It seemed like so much to remember! A big copy of *The Night Before Christmas* hung there at one point as well and we worked on memorizing that. Memory work was emphasized in education and my father wanted to be sure I had a head start!

In 1936 when Edward VIII succeeded George V, Dad taught me the names of the new king. I think there was always a bit of something between my father and the teacher, Mr. Goodyear. He had come to St. George's as a new teacher many years before and Uncle Hilliard's girlfriend had jilted him for the new teacher. She reportedly told Uncle Hilliard, my father's brother, that he would never be anything but a fisherman, and I guess it stuck in my father's craw, to use a common expression of the time. I'm sure he knew the teacher would get around to the new king and it wasn't long before he did. When he asked the one-room school of probably thirty if anyone knew the name of the new king, little Cavell was ready and put up her hand.

"Yes," said Mr. Goodyear, "what is the new king's name, Cavell?"

Out came, "Edward Albert Christian George Andrew Patrick David."

I don't remember Mr. Goodyear's reaction but when I related it later to my father, his smile said it all.

One day Dad came home with a big parcel that had come in the mail. Parcels were a big deal in our house, especially one coming to the post office. Usually they were from Eaton's mail order in Toronto and meant new stockings or underwear. This time it was an Aladdin lamp. Why did we need a new lamp? The one that was fastened on the wall over the kitchen table did the same job of illuminating the room as did everyone else's that I knew. This must be something special! Dad filled the font, fastened the mesh mantle and lit it in a swoosh. What a light—brighter than any I had ever seen! It seemed that the whole room took on a brightness lighter than day. And it was perfect for schoolwork!

There was a contradiction in my father's attitude to education. In spite of taking such an interest in his daughters' education, he had another deeply held opinion that one day resulted in an argument between him and my mother. This was scary because normally there was never any disagreement that I heard. It had to do with education for girls. Dad argued that girls didn't need as much education as boys, which was a widely-held position embraced by many families. In hard times it often happened that girls stopped school to help support the family. It was known as "going into service" with a more well-off family. Also, sometimes girls were kept home to help in the house, especially when there were large numbers of young children.

I heard my dad say that girls didn't need higher education because they would marry and be staying at home whereas boys would be the breadwinners. My mother disagreed strongly. We children weren't allowed to disagree or "talk back" and here she was doing just that! This must be very important! Her position was that girls also needed an education and must be given that opportunity to develop themselves. Besides, girls should have an education to fall back on if they found themselves supporting a family. It seemed pretty reasonable to me and I never forgot it!

Mom had only one year of high school and I never knew why, but it obviously felt like a handicap to her. Her only sister, Bessie, four years older, finished high school and went to summer school to train as a teacher. In some ways, I think Mother felt the lack of education keenly. Two or three years after this exchange she was a widow with very little income and no back up.

Dad held to another widely-held belief that the teacher was always right. This belief didn't seem to recognize that some days the teacher could be out of sorts due to other reasons and dispensed the strap more liberally than usual. Many children were told that if the teacher gave them the strap, they would get an equal number of strokes when they got home (meant to improve discipline, no doubt). Shortly after I started school, Dad took Phyllis and me to the work shed where he showed us a belt made from a section of reins he had readied for us. He told us what it was for and that he was going to give us a taste of it. When he gave us each a whack on the hand with it I was flabbergasted and heartbroken. My gentle father whom I regarded as my protector was hurting me for nothing. Only once did Mr. Goodyear give me the strap when it was entirely unexpected. It was either for not having finished my work or for not having done it correctly. That one whack of the strap really hurt my hand, but it hurt my heart more.

After supper when the lamp was lit, Dad sat at one end of the kitchen table beside the kitchen door and read the paper. Phyllis and I washed our hands and face in the white enamel basin placed at child-height on a chair and were told to push up our sleeves and wash right up to our elbows. Whoever finished first was the first to kneel at Dad's knee to say our prayers before bed. This was serious business as the four-lined verse finished with, "If I should die before I wake, I pray the Lord my soul to take." What a thought to go to bed with! I used to have trouble getting to sleep for I thought there was a good chance of never waking up!

THE DOLL CRADLE

The Christmas I was three, I got a beautiful doll cradle, a replica of the one my baby sister, Phyllis, was sleeping in (one which Dad had slept in, as had I). The cradle was probably two-thirds the size of a regular one. It was made of dark stained wood and sat on the floor on rockers with a hood that was supposed to keep draughts from the baby's head. (This was necessary, I would think, as the houses were built on the ground with no basement and the floors were the coldest, draftiest places in houses with no central heating.) Anyway, my dad had made this cradle and kept it a secret until it appeared under the Christmas tree on Christmas morning complete with a doll in fine new clothes.

I was so happy to have a cradle of my own for my doll. For what had seemed ages I hadn't been able to find my old doll, Lucy, much as I searched for her. She was the only doll I had, and I had been feeling guilty at losing her for I was supposed to look after my things. Now Lucy was back, lying in the new cradle in new clothes that my mother had made while I slept. When I didn't recognize her, I was so embarrassed! The cradle remains one of my most treasured possessions. On its underside, my dad wrote in heavy pencil:

Christmas, 1930
Cavell, may you be a good little girl always and
we won't ever forget you
Santa Claus

It was only when I was reunited with the cradle sixty years later that I saw the inscription for the first time that I can remember. It had always been "the cradle" that was played with by the youngest niece. Carol Squires rescued it for me when Aunt Bessie Vardy's house was being emptied after she died.

OUR HOMELIFE

My cousin, Audrey, was four years older than I and was my best friend. She lived in a big grey house up through our field and across the road and would often walk down to our place, much to our delight. Things were always more exciting when Audrey came. Once, after gathering the eggs from the henhouse, she persuaded us to pick and eat the peas in the vegetable garden that Mom had said were for Sunday dinner. When Mom discovered our hiding place in the pea patch, Audrey was sent packing and Phyllis and I to the house!

Audrey loved the beach as much as we did, and we played there for hours. She was also the person who took me to school on my first day and her family gave me the small desk that I used in school.

The only supplies needed when I started school in 1933 was a slate and a slate pencil. The slate was exactly that: a piece of slate around 9x6 inches surrounded by a wooden frame. The slate pencil was shaped like a wooden pencil, but thinner, and pointed at one end, which made grey marks on the slate. We used it as we would a lead pencil for letters and numerals. To clean off all the writing, we used a rag dampened by soapy water carried from home in a small bottle. Some kids used spit and their sleeve!

As we graduated through grades, we got to use lead pencils and paper "scribblers," and then we learned how to write with pen and ink. This was a big deal, for now we were considered responsible enough to handle ink, which filled the inkwell, a small container sunk into the upper corner of the desk. The pen was a pen nib attached to a slim wooden handle that was inclined to drip on one's work if not properly loaded. To keep the work from smudging we used a blotter, a stiff rectangle of paper with an absorbent side. Fountain pens came later and were much easier because they only had to be loaded occasionally. Ballpoints were new around thirty years later.

Reading this makes me feel a bit like a relic from another age!!

A MEMORABLE CHRISTMAS

The summer that Audrey was twelve her mother died. Her sister, Reatha, had come from Toronto and was stern, so Mom, to make it more fun for Audrey, invited her to spend Christmas Eve overnight with Phyllis and me. It was the only sleepover we had ever had, and we were excited in the days leading up to it. There were three of us in our bed, and Audrey kept us awake (and amusing herself) by scratching at the window telling us it was Santa Claus! Finally, we were all asleep and our parents could get down to business!

It was their custom to prepare everything after we went to sleep. The tree would be brought in and set up in the dining room complete with colourful glass ornaments and real candles, which were lit for the unveiling. When Mom and Dad opened the dining room door the tree was magical! Santa was supposed to have done the whole thing, but it was fun. So was unwrapping our gifts. Gifts were few and usually a piece of clothing and a book.

One year just before Christmas, I was upstairs rummaging in one of the spare rooms where there was a trunk. Without thinking of Christmas, I lifted the lid just to see what might be there and found to my great surprise a pair of winter boots! Of course, I tried them on, and they fit perfectly. I ran downstairs to let Mom know what was in the trunk. Without batting an eye, she said that Santa had such a load this year that he had dropped by asking if she had any room until he could pick them on his way to the North Pole later. She said we shouldn't let anybody know as it was a secret. Secrets were a big deal, and I never breathed a word to anyone. Imagine my surprise on Christmas morning when an exact pair were under the tree for me. Santa had decided to give them to me, and I was delighted!

It must have been around this time that I asked Dad if Santa had a wife. When he said "yes" I asked him what her name was. With a straight face he told me it was "Mary." I can remember saying, "Oh, just like Mom's name!"

One Christmas morning Dad played a joke on us. We had been listening to stories of Santa for weeks and had partially memorized *The Night Before Christmas*. Naturally we were all hyped up, and as we were opening our stockings we suddenly heard bells! This was a new sound in our house so it must be true! Santa must be on the roof of our house just as the poem said! We rushed to the window expecting to see Santa and his reindeer on the roof just like our picture on the wall, but there was no Santa! So sad, too late! Dad went into the bedroom and turned off the alarm clock! It was the first time we had ever heard it for Dad never needed one! His plan had worked and afterwards when alone my parents must have had a good laugh.

I had a doll, Bessie, given to me by my Aunt Bessie for my first Christmas. This doll came out only at Christmas and was kept for "good." I still have her. She is an "Eaton's Beauty" and her eyes open when she sits up and close when she lies down just as they did over ninety years ago. Keeping something for "good" was a practice that was supposed to teach children to look after their things. This practice also applied to clothing where one outfit was kept as "good" and was only worn on Sundays. Even men who were not churchgoers made sure they had a suit to be buried in! Houses had a best room that was used only for funerals and the minister's visit. All other entertaining was done in the kitchen, a big room that was always warm and also served as a gathering place.

It must have been the Christmas that I was eight and Phyllis six when we received a checkers game. We were entranced when Dad showed us how to play. We played endlessly and it wasn't long before Phyllis was beating the pants off me—her whoops of delight really bugged me. After all, I was two years older and therefore supposed to be smarter. My interest in checkers faded!

INSIDE WORK

Our mother worked hard. The house was large with six bedrooms upstairs and two down off the kitchen, the warmest room in the house. The upstairs rooms were unused except for a visitor, boarder or occasionally a helper. Usually, Mom did all the housework herself but on occasion, if she were unwell or when Shirley was born, "a girl" would be hired to help with the work. I remember one "girl" who dressed in black. Although very young, she was a widow and just before she came to us, her baby had died also. Her name was Amelia and she was very nice, but she coughed a lot. Our parents were worried about tuberculosis, which was prevalent, and they let her go. It was sad for her and for us.

Phyllis and I didn't like another "girl" named Edna very much, and the feeling was reciprocated. This was probably because of the way we treated her. Shirley was a baby at the time, and there was lots to do. Edna had trouble getting out of bed in the mornings and was late in the kitchen where she was needed. One day I heard Dad say, no doubt remembering his army experiences, "What she needs is a cup of cold water in the face." Ever ready to be helpful, I quietly went upstairs and did just that! There was a scream, and I bolted downstairs where I proudly told them what I had done! Of course, I was reprimanded and no doubt my father learned to watch what he said around me! I'm sure they must have had a good laugh later.

All the washing was done on Monday and hung out to dry all year round. In the winter after an hour or so, it would be frozen on the line. The frosty air continued to dry it somewhat and the sun made it white. To help with the whitening was something called "bluing," which when added to the rinse water actually did make a difference. Bluing came in small, hard blue cakes an inch or so square and one would be put in a small square of cloth, tied with a string and swished around in the final rinse water. Starching would also be done after drying. My mother made a thick flour paste into which she poured boiling water and the shirt collars, dresser scarves and anything that needed to look spiffy!

When the frozen clothes came inside in the winter, they would be hung around the stove to dry and also on the banisters upstairs on either side of the stairwell. Tuesday was ironing day and there was lots to iron for everything was pure cotton—no synthetics—and was very wrinkled. Electricity hadn't come to St. George's yet so the flatirons had to be heated on the stove. Our mother had three so while one was being used and cooling down, the others were getting hot on the wood-stove. Phyllis and I learned to use them later on and got to be pretty good at it.

Mom baked bread every week and we children made sure to be around when it came out of the oven. The minute it was turned out of the pans, Mom cut a slice of the hot bread, covered it with our own homemade butter and topped it with sweet molasses. What a treat!

Sometimes we added molasses to a glass of milk for a homemade milkshake and sometimes people would use it to sweeten their tea. We always bought it by the gallon!

Mom's baking also included cakes, special ones she baked for a sale at the church or at the church "Ladies Aid." These were always made with a special flour—"Swan's Down" cake flour—which made for a higher, lighter cake than those from bread flour. It was no easy feat as she had to build the fire in the wood-stove such that the heat would be just right and stay that way while the cake was baking. It was one of her few extravaganzas and she was known for her cakes!

In haying season, she would be outside to help spread the hay in the morning and to rake it back into heaps (pooks) at night. In lobster season, she joined in the canning operation at the factory.

She also made all our clothes on a treadle sewing machine, which took days. As we grew, both Phyllis and I needed a new coat every other year. Mom made them with a deep hem that could be let down in the second year. Phyllis never wore passed down clothes, which, considering the circumstances after our dad died, indicated Mom's deep understanding of Phyllis' feelings.

Mom was the disciplinarian in the family and we received many a hard smack on the hand when she felt it was warranted. We never did! And we weren't allowed to cry! That was hard and even as grown-ups Phyllis and I continued to "bottle it up."

These were hard times for families in the Depression and Mom certainly knew how to stretch a dollar and maintain the image of the family's success. She was the perfect partner for our father. He had waited for a partner until he was forty-four!

STARTING TO GROW UP

We also had chores and I was the first to be started on these as Phyllis was younger. That didn't sit too well with me, and I was not too happy about it as she was pretty competitive about everything else!

The fall I started school it became my job to fill the wood box before dark. The woodpile was a few yards from the back door and in order to make as few trips as possible I carried as big an arm full as I could. Mom kept telling me not to carry as much, but I didn't pay attention. Those armloads were pretty heavy—much too heavy judging by the scoliosis I developed later.

Another chore that came my way was to sweep the kitchen floor with a new broom that was the smallest I had ever seen. The floor in question were the parts that weren't covered by the hooked mats and I guess I missed a lot in the beginning. I didn't get away with it though and before long my work passed inspection!

Setting the table for supper and picking the peas for Sunday dinner were also chores that interfered with my important play time! Having to do these things seemed like a hardship but now I realize it was good training, for I developed an attitude toward work that made my life easier later on.

I must have been seven or eight and it was lobster canning time. We were all down at the factory. I was sent home ahead of time to put another piece of wood on the fire and set the table. I did this and to really show what I could do, I decided to put dinner on the table too. The pot of beans that had been baking in the oven all day was ready, so I began to take it out. The pot was much heavier than I expected, and a lot of the dinner went on the floor! I felt terrible and expected that I was in big trouble for sure! But contrary to form Mom said very little. I think she understood and didn't want to turn off that enthusiasm for taking on new things. Thanks Mom.

MOM'S SEWING

Mom made all our clothes on Grandma Butt's treadle sewing machine. It was fascinating to see Mom's feet pumping away on the treadle under the machine while the piston went up and down on top. There was just something about the movement that attracted small children. I can't remember doing it, but I remember being warned about making the treadle go up and down when the machine was dropped into its cradle to become a table. Without being engaged by cloth, the needle went up and down in the same place and got the thread and tension snarled up. Shirley got into the fun once and caused a lot of trouble.

Our dresses were cut by memory or intuition. Once sewn up, the final shaping around the neck and armholes was done with a pair of scissors. And we couldn't move while this was going on! When we were really young some of Dad's old shirts saw a second life as our everyday dresses, which were tied at the back to make them fit!

One special outfit I remember was made of persimmon-coloured silk and had an embroidered spray of flowers on the front just above the hem. Phyllis and I wore these dresses on our holiday to Corner Brook one summer. I have a picture of Phyllis and one of me taken by Bob Milley who lived with us. We loved those dresses and only wore them for special occasions. Mom dry cleaned them with gasoline out behind the house much to Dad's concern!

When Shirley was a few months old Mom and Dad made tod equivalent of a Jolly Jumper based on a picture in the Eaton's catalogue. Dad made the frame and Mom sewed the seat out of blue denim. It had four sides, the back being higher than the others, and in the front were the two spaces for the baby's legs to protrude. It hung by four heavy cords suspended from a heavy spring screwed into the ceiling by the stove next to the hall door. Mom had been concerned about the baby crawling around on the cold floor but now Shirley could spend some time in the swing and be in a warmer spot. Phyllis and I loved it too. We could bounce Shirley all over the place and hear her squealing until Mom could stand it no longer!

THE GREAT OUTDOORS

Outside was where the really interesting things happened, and I loved being outdoors. Besides, it was where Dad was, and I loved being with him. He built things and fixed things with hammer and saw, and I was always on his heels when he worked around home. He talked to me and let me find and hold things for him. I felt so important and happy, and I felt he was my friend.

One spring when I was around six or seven, with my "help" he built a smoke house down on the bank beside the cellar overlooking the water. It seemed the construction went on for days and, of course, I helped! He dug a hole in the bank that could be accessed from below and built the smoke house above it with a grillwork to keep animals out but let the excess smoke from inside escape. It had rows of poles over which the split salmon and herring were hung. I don't remember how many days that the smoker needed to be kept burning but the final results were worth it. The kippers and smoked salmon were out of this world!

By August the grass was ready to be mowed and that was a big day. For weeks we had been cautioned not to run in the long grass for it was very hard to cut when it was flattened. This was a job that Dad did with a scythe, which had a long, slightly S-shaped handle that he grasped by two protruding bits and swung in long rhythmical strokes. The three-foot blade was attached at the bottom of the handle and with each swing the mown grass grew in beautiful rows across the field.

Once, as Dad was mowing the long grass, he uncovered a bird's nest and called us over to see it. It was the first bird's nest we had ever seen. We were enchanted and visited it for what seemed like weeks until the eggs hatched, and the birds grew up and flew away.

Ours was a large field of about four acres, and after the first day of mowing, Dad's back really ached. Mom brought out the Minard's Liniment, a powerful smelling product that was a household staple, and rubbed it into his sore muscles. Mowing must have been harder for him than for most men because of his war injury. His long back muscle had been almost severed by a piece of shrapnel that also took off a part of the vertebra and caused him to have that distinctive walk.

Everybody worked at "making" the hay. With some luck, the rain held off and made the drying process faster. During the day, the mown grass was spread around to dry in the sun, and before the dew fell it was raked and stacked into "pooks" against the dew (or rain).

One day when Mom was taking time out to nurse baby Shirley behind one of these low haystacks, I thought I would surprise her. The one who was surprised was me! As I threw myself over the pook, the hayfork that she had stuck into it for safety skewered me in the leg. I landed beside her with a scream, my leg in the air with the fork hanging by the neat two-inch stitch it had taken in the front of my lower leg. There was no blood, and this worried my parents even more as there was an ever present danger of lockjaw in the days before tetanus shots. My cousin, Effie, who had come home from Detroit with her friend "Phyllis the Nurse" was sent for. I was a hero for a few days as we followed Phyllis' advice to stay in bed and wear a bread poultice to draw out any infection.

The process of stacking at night and spreading in the morning would be repeated for several days before the hay was considered dry. Then the man with the horse came to take it to the barn where it fed Daisy the cow all winter. But the best part of all was jumping in the hay once it was inside. This was forbidden, but the danger of spontaneous combustion seemed remote, and we did it anyhow when we didn't think we would be caught!

One year we had an abundance of hay, and Dad decided to sell some. He rigged up a balance for weighing it near the cow's stall and tacked a piece of cardboard onto one of the posts with a pencil hanging beside it. As each load was weighed and the long columns of what looked like 1s grew, I couldn't resist it any longer. I took the pencil and joined the 1s together—carefully. When Dad came to tally up the loads, all he could see was one long vertical pencil line! I don't remember if I got a whack on the bottom or not, but I was certainly sent packing to the house!

SUNDAYS

Sunday was our day to socialize. Going to church was a big event and Mom got the dinner on before she left. Sunday dinner was usually the same and was our favourite meal—it still is mine. The salt beef would have been soaked overnight to remove a lot of the salt and put into fresh water at breakfast time on the roaring woodstove. When it was time to leave, Mom added the turnip, cabbage and potatoes in that order and moved it to the back of the stove so it wouldn't overcook before we got home. She was very proud of this strategy for she held that lots of women used the excuse of cooking Sunday dinner not to go to church!

When the dandelions were big enough but before coming into bloom, they went into the pot instead of cabbage for a delicious spring treat. The day before, Phyllis and I would have been sent into the field to cut them off at the root. We didn't like this job much and before long would have convinced ourselves that we had enough and come back to proudly present them to Mom. We couldn't get away with it though, and she'd send us out to finish the job. It was worth the effort. The dandelions were delicious, and we were proud to have contributed to the family dinner.

We weren't an overtly religious family. Going to church was something we just did and what we heard we tried to put into practice through the week. The Butts were Anglican—or "Church of England" as it was termed—when they first lived on Sandy Point. Somewhere in the mid 1800s when John Wesley was preaching his vision for a less formal religion in Britain and the United States, his message reached Sandy Point through my Great-grandfather Solomon who had immigrated from Exploits on the north coast. A small group of "Wesleyans" was formed, and they met in each other's homes. By the time my great-grandfather and his sons made the move across the water to St. George's, he was one of the lay preachers. Sometime later the Wesleyans adopted the name "Methodists." Great-grandfather Solomon was one of the founders of the new church, the first Methodist church (now United Church) to be built in St. George's. He was involved in building the church, and his diary is still in existence enumerating the supplies and how much they cost.

It must have been some time after the move from Sandy Point that the new church was built because when his wife, my Great-grandmother Judith Ann (née Parsons, from Sandy Point) died, she was buried in their field. Her headstone, which also commemorates their son, James, who was lost at sea, is still visible behind some Butt houses to the east of Arnold Morris' lane.

Death was always present in a seafaring community and was such a fact of life that many elderly men made their own coffins. Great-grandpa Solomon made his and, I'm told, kept it behind his bedroom door!

My father sat on the board of the church, and one of his last acts in 1936 was to lay the foundation for the new church being built across the road. He worked into the late fall, and as the weather became colder Mother worried he would get chilled. She sent me up with hot food and I stayed a while to watch how he laid out the long sills following the lines he had squared and marked with string and pegs. As usual I was his helper and handed him the tools he needed. Would it be immodest of me to claim to have had a hand in the building of the church?!

In church, my father liked to sing loudly but not as loudly as his brothers, Uncle Hilliard and Uncle Alfred. We sat on the right about two or three rows from the front, and my uncles' families sat on the left a few rows behind us. The Butts must have boosted the vocal power by quite a bit! They complained that the hymns were played too fast and asked to have the pace slowed as they were used to, but it didn't do any good. Perhaps this was because the organist was Mrs. Goodyear, the teacher's wife who had had an "understanding" with my Uncle Hilliard as I mentioned earlier. Mrs. Goodyear had another connection to our family that rankled some. When my very elderly Great-grandfather Solomon lost my great-grandmother some years before, Delia Goodyear arranged for her widowed grandmother from the south coast to housekeep for him. It was a "shotgun" wedding though not for the usual reasons! "Shotgun" in the sense that it was very rushed—only a few months after his wife's death. His son, my Grandfather Nathaniel, was away on a trading trip to Halifax and New York when they were married and, to the town's amazement and probable approval, when his schooner sailed into St. George's not long after, he was flying his flag at half-mast indicating bereavement.

GRANDPA NATHANIEL

My grandfather, whom I never knew, died many years before I was born but I heard many stories about him.

He was a seafarer with his own schooner and had earned his sea captain designation as a young man. Most of his adult life was spent on the sea trading along the Canadian and American seaboard.

Grandpa Nathaniel was quite a strong character, upright and honest to a fault. Uncle Stan used to tell a story about him. Grandpa Nathaniel's son, Uncle Hilliard, was one of the crew and about to be married, so he had been shopping for furnishings in Halifax. He had bought their wedding china there and was bringing it home to his bride. He was also hoping to evade the import tax due on all goods being brought into Newfoundland. So, when his father's schooner was being unloaded, Uncle Hilliard was paying special attention to a certain barrel as it swung off the deck and onto the wharf. Just as the barrel reached the wharf and was suspended high above it, his father, Captain Nat, ordered the load to be dropped. The effect was devastating. The barrel split and broken dishes went in all directions. I understand that no words were spoken as Uncle Hilliard and the crew cleaned up the mess. My grandfather would have no part of smuggling. In St. John's, the port with facilities for collecting import taxes from all ships entering the harbour, it was no problem, but in all other villages or towns—"outports"— collecting import tax was the responsibility of the captain. Grandpa took this responsibility seriously!

Grandpa Nathaniel also believed in the old injunction "spare the rod and spoil the child" and used it freely in their home. The children feared him and were not that happy to see him return, according to Uncle Stan. Neither were they spared as teenagers and young adults. Apparently he gave Uncle Alfred a whipping the night before his wedding!

All of his sons went to sea with him and learned seamanship under his command. None of them wanted to spend more time than they had to on his vessels for he was a hard taskmaster, and none pursued that profession.

He was exacting when training crew, which was necessary for safety. In the days before power when wind was the only propellant, sailors had to "know the ropes" that controlled each sail and to be quick about it; it could mean life or death. Most sailors knew which captain they could trust with their lives and which to avoid. Grandpa Nat could always assemble an experienced crew. He would have spent years as a sailor before studying for the exacting exams required to achieve the captain designation. Captains knew how to get the most out of their vessels and their sails, and how to read the weather, the sea and the tides.

Winters meant fewer trips at sea and more time to attend to matters at home. Though he was a Protestant he was good friends with the Catholic Bishop McNeil. This was at a time when there wasn't much mixing of the two religions, but they shared a deep friendship. The Bishop's Palace (as his residence was known) was still on Sandy Point, which for many years had been the main centre of the population. It was now needed in St. George's where the main Catholic population lived, including the bishop, and my grandfather was hired to move it across the water. It must have been in winter as Grandpa would have been on the water in his schooner as soon as the ice was out, and in any case the job would have been easier when the ice was good and thick.

Sometimes houses were moved by attaching empty barrels to their base and floating them to their new homes, but in the bishop's case the large house was likely moved on rollers when ice and frozen ground made it easier. Moving heavy objects was done in the same way by boat or house: slim logs were cut and placed under the object to be moved. Block and tackle would have been attached to the house and then everybody pulled. In some cases, horses would be involved with the pulling, and as the rear log rolled out the back it was quickly placed in front and the rolling continued until the house was in the desired place! It must have been a big event in the small town and there was likely no lack of pullers and pushers! Block and tackle were used on land and sea. The wooden block with its internal rollers reduced the effort needed to lift heavy objects on land, and at sea it was essential for raising fifty foot sails!

The Bishop's Palace is still in place high on the hill and is now a B&B! Bishop Neil McNeil later became archbishop of Toronto and later archbishop of Vancouver.

Much of my grandfather's life was spent on the water, and trading and fishing were his business. At one point he owned several schooners and besides the trading along the eastern seaboard of North America, his enterprises included the Labrador summer fishery. Sometimes he sent a schooner "down" to the Labrador for the summer fishery under another captain. To go to the Labrador was always "down" even though it was north! Even when I was a girl, it was always referred to as "the" Labrador. Nobody knows why but it was probably referring to "the" Labrador fishery, which occurred along the coast.

The interior of Labrador was known only by the indigenous people at that time. There was no mining, electricity dams or towns. The villages along the coast were mostly indigenous—"Indian" in the south and "Inuit" farther north.

The story goes that one summer there was a fierce storm on the Labrador with much loss of life and cargo. At the station agent's, which was also where telegrams came in, grandpa learned that his vessel had been lost. Thinking the boat wasn't insured, he trudged up the hill to where his old friend the bishop resided and sunk into a chair saying, "Neil, I've been ruined." Making his way home with the bad news, he found that his daughter, Ruth, had indeed insured the vessel and the loss wasn't as bad as it could have been!

Most years, the Labrador fishery meant Grandpa Nat would be away from April to October, and when he returned he must have felt it his duty to straighten out the family! There were four daughters and six sons. Grandma produced a new baby every two years like most of the women she knew. Grandma had sixteen pregnancies, ten of whom lived. Though grandpa spent a lot of his time away, he was certainly home long enough to keep the family increasing! The kids were Solomon (died in infancy), Hilliard, Wallace, Stanley, Samuel, Alfred, Talbot, Diana (Sis), Mary, Ruth, and Edith (died of the Spanish Flu, which she contracted in Nova Scotia where she was buying her trousseau in 1918).

Grandpa was also a temperance man at the time when it became a movement. It was a misnomer because it actually insisted on abstinence, not temperance. It did a lot to reduce the hardships suffered by families of drinking fathers. Capt. Nat built the temperance hall (which later became the school) and many speakers enthusiastically belted out the message from its platform. When the fervour was built to a certain point, young men were exhorted to "Take the Pledge" and many did, especially Capt. Nat's sons! My father did. One wonders how much coercion entered into their signing!

My father kept his pledge, and it was put to the test later in the war. The Royal Newfoundland Regiment received most of their training in England and at one point my father was assigned to the "wet" canteen where the soldiers could get beer. My dad refused to accept the assignment even though to go against orders was unthinkable—refusing an order meant severe repercussions with punishment involved. But he stood his ground and he was put on charge and brought before the commanding officer. When asked why he had refused, he simply stated that he had pledged to have nothing to do with alcohol. His principles would not allow him to go against his sworn oath and also his conscience would not allow him to serve alcohol to mothers' sons who would in many cases be going against their earlier promise. The colonel said he had to respect Dad's position and told the duty officer to assign Dad to another area!

DEATH AS PART OF LIFE

Our church was set back from the road on the south end of the town and looked out to sea. It was white clapboard and boasted a porch topped by what would have been a steeple had it been finished. It looked quite good behind its white picket fence surrounded by the headstones. When we went into the cemetery we were surrounded by family and friends' headstones, and we soon learned who was who. Our grandparents, Susan and Nathaniel, were there, as was Audrey's mother, Aunt Sarah. The graves of our grandparents' four young children who died during an epidemic of erysipelas were against the east wall of the church. There were also the graves of Aunt Mary's two children, many neighbours and the many we didn't know who had been lost at sea.

There were graves on Sandy Point, too, that had significance for us. It was where our Grandma Susan's people were buried. She was the daughter of George Pieroway and Mary Ann Dalton. Her brother, Uncle Joe Pieroway, still lived in Sandy Point.

Sometime in June, Flower Sunday was held, and we would go over from St. George's to attend the service. Mom brought dahlias she bought from Mrs. LeRoux up the road every Sunday for our own church service. The graves were cleaned up in advance and looked well cared for when the flowers were placed there lovingly. These were graves of people I didn't know, and I found it hard to relate to them, but they were family to Dad, and he told us who they were.

As children we went to funerals with our parents and also went to people's homes to pay our respects when somebody died. The body would be laid out in their coffin in the parlour and we would all visit it there. It was the way things were done then, and we grew up knowing death was part of life. There were always incidents of drownings, even of children.

One Easter, it must have been Easter Sunday, Phyllis and I piled into bed with Mom and Dad, something we were allowed to do occasionally. On this particular occasion, we were introduced to the Easter story. I thought it was the worst thing I had ever heard—hanging a live human being on a cross to die. It haunted me for years, and I sure couldn't see its connection to me. It must have been when I was around six that we got into the explanation of God. Before this I had simply accepted the term, but now I wanted to know where God was and who he was. My parent's explanation—God is everywhere and knows everything—didn't make sense of a being who was referred to as a "Him." And where was heaven anyway? Was this person there? I guess my parents felt they needed reinforcements and asked the minister to talk to me. I felt a bit embarrassed to be singled out, and when he left I was as confused as ever.

I have always felt that a more appropriate pronoun for this Universal Power is "It." "It" being a respectful term for the power that animates all things and keeps everything in the universe in balance and functioning (except when Man gets in the way!).

SUNDAYS AND EVERYDAY RELIGION

On Sunday, Phyllis and I would be sent to our bedroom to get into our best clothes, the ones saved for Sundays. Mom and Dad would get dressed in their bedroom, and Mom took a lot longer than Dad.

We loved to watch them getting dressed. Dad would be shaving at the little washstand just inside the bedroom door. We were fascinated to see him strop his open-bladed straight razor on the belt that hung at the side. After testing the edge for sharpness with his thumb and repeating the process a couple of times, he began to take long slow strokes across his face. We had been cautioned about the razor's sharpness and how it could cut one badly. We were in awe at how brave he was! He donned his collarless shirt and began attaching one of the loose collars he kept in a small round box on the dresser. A "stud" fastened it to his shirt and after the tie was in place he was ready and left the room.

Now we could give all our attention to Mom! This was much more complicated! She stepped into her corset, which all women of that time wore when they dressed up. It was worn over an undergarment and extended from under the bust right down over the hips and was tightened with laces at the back that ran its whole length. It held everything in and gave a compact, slimmer line. When the corset came off later, the skin that had been compressed into folds under this garment itched and there was a good deal of rubbing of the affected spots.

With her navy serge suit, she wore a yellow silk blouse, which hung outside her skirt as far as her hips in the style of the twenties. It was probably the one she had been married in. She fastened the cuffs with her gold cufflinks that bore her initials: "MEN"—Mary Emma Norman. With her blue hat she looked gorgeous. Before the hat came her jewelry. Around her neck she hung a gold piece on a chain Dad had given to her on their wedding day. It was a ten-dollar gold piece with a scroll-like mount attaching it to the gold chain. It was also inscribed with her initials. She used to amuse us by pressing it into the flesh of her chest and taking her finger off it. As if by magic it continued to stay there for what seemed like ages before falling off.

Next came her red fox fur, which she draped around her shoulders. This was the latest fashion in Toronto when she had left a few years before, and I knew no other mother with one. We were fascinated by the way a spring allowed the jaws to open and snap shut on another clip farther along the body so that the fox seemed to wrap itself around her shoulders with the tail hanging down one side. I never saw her wear it after we left St. George's.

Sunday School was held at the church from two to three o'clock. We didn't like going back so soon although the Bible stories were interesting. Anyway, we had no choice. Once I won a book called *Poor Men Who Made Us Rich* for not having missed any Sundays. It was written by Archer Wallace and was about Mozart, Spinoza, Goldsmith and others. The stories were inspirational and interesting and were written for children by the same person whose name appeared on our Sunday School papers as editor. He was a family friend, well-loved in the community and came from Toronto to spend his summers in Newfoundland at Boswarlos on the Port au Port Peninsula. He had spent his probationary time in St. George's as a young minister from England, had made many friends and had fallen in love with that part of Newfoundland.

Dad lived his religion in his everyday dealings with people, quoting the Bible to my mother when he came home without his new rubber boots. "Am I my brother's keeper?" he said when Mom asked where they were. That morning, Jack Samms, a fisherman with a large family in Flat Bay, was really up against it and had come to Dad for help. Jack wanted to fish for the summer but didn't have any way of getting what he needed, so he approached my father. Dad gave him fishing supplies as well as food essentials so he could fish all summer. Although Dad was not a merchant, they agreed on the usual arrangement between fishermen and a merchant who had the connections for selling the dried fish in the fall. When the fish was sold and they settled up, the fisherman would have enough left to support his family until the next year—if it had been a good fishing season!

Because Jack's boots were in tatters, Dad had taken off his own boots and given them to him. Dad's boots were new and when Mom saw what he was wearing when he came home for dinner she had something to say about it. Anything new was hard to come by in our house. I remember Dad describing how hard-up that family was and how he saw it as his duty to help out. I wasn't sure what Dad meant when he said, "Am I my brother's keeper?" I wondered which brother he was talking about—was Jack Samms his brother too? If so, why didn't he have the same last name?

The same question arose again when Jack Joe, a local First Nations man spent a day working on our woodpile. I was fascinated by his dark skin. A few weeks later when my attitude needed correcting about something or other, Mom impressed on me that all men are brothers. I asked if Jack Joe was my brother too. When she said, "Yes, everyone," I was puzzled and remarked that he didn't look like anyone in our family!

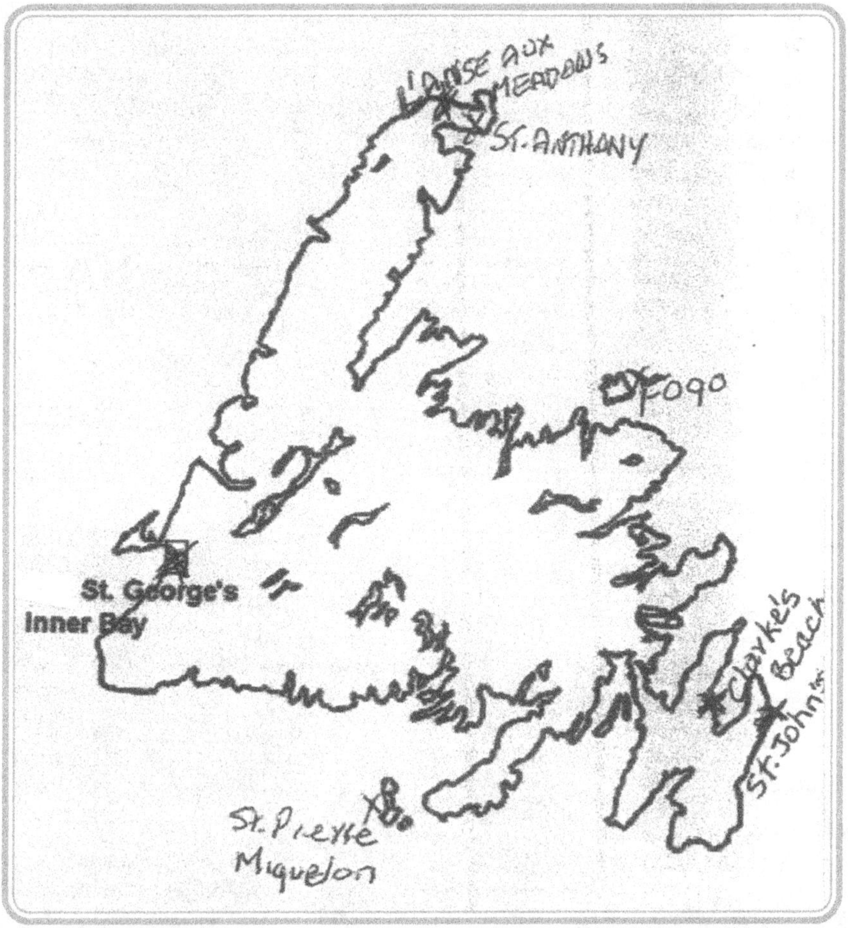

Map of Newfoundland showing St.George's and Clarke's Beach.

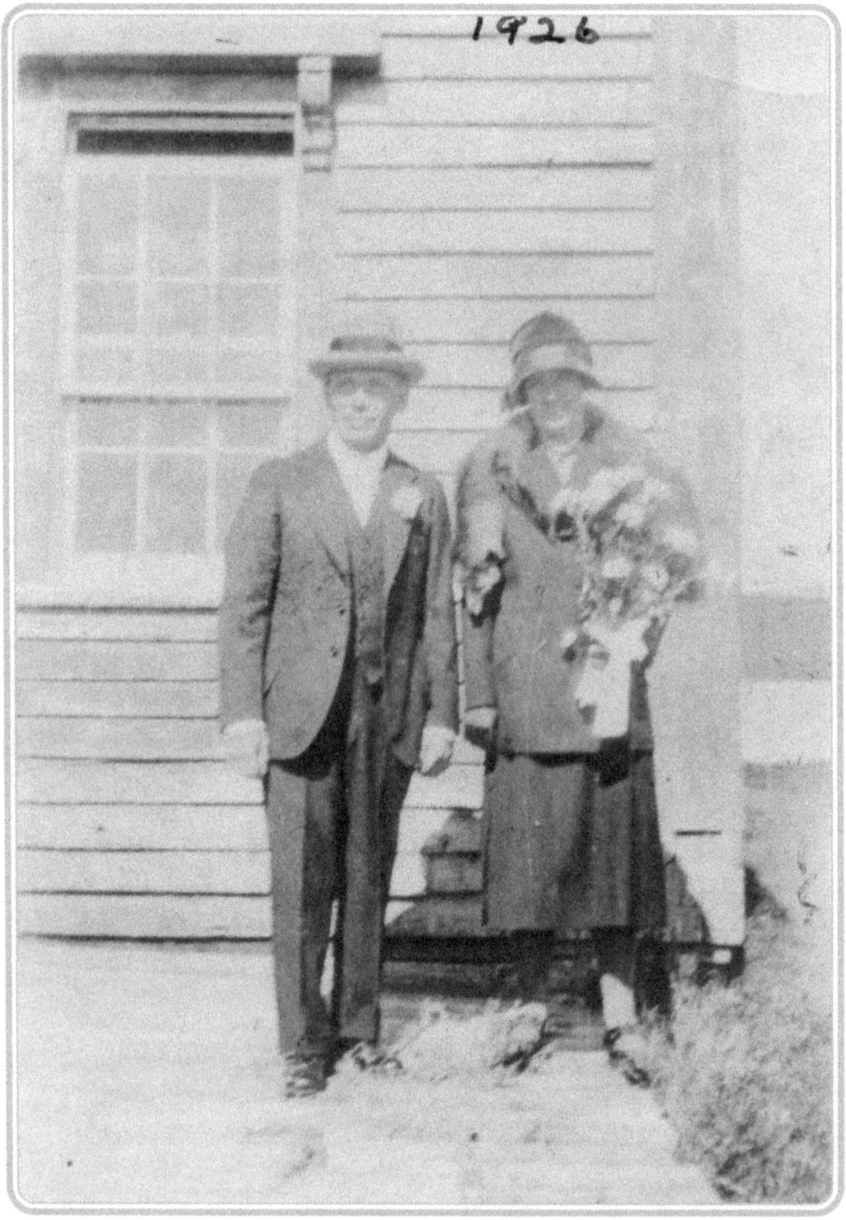

Parents' Samuel Butt and Mary Norman wedding, Sept 20, 1926

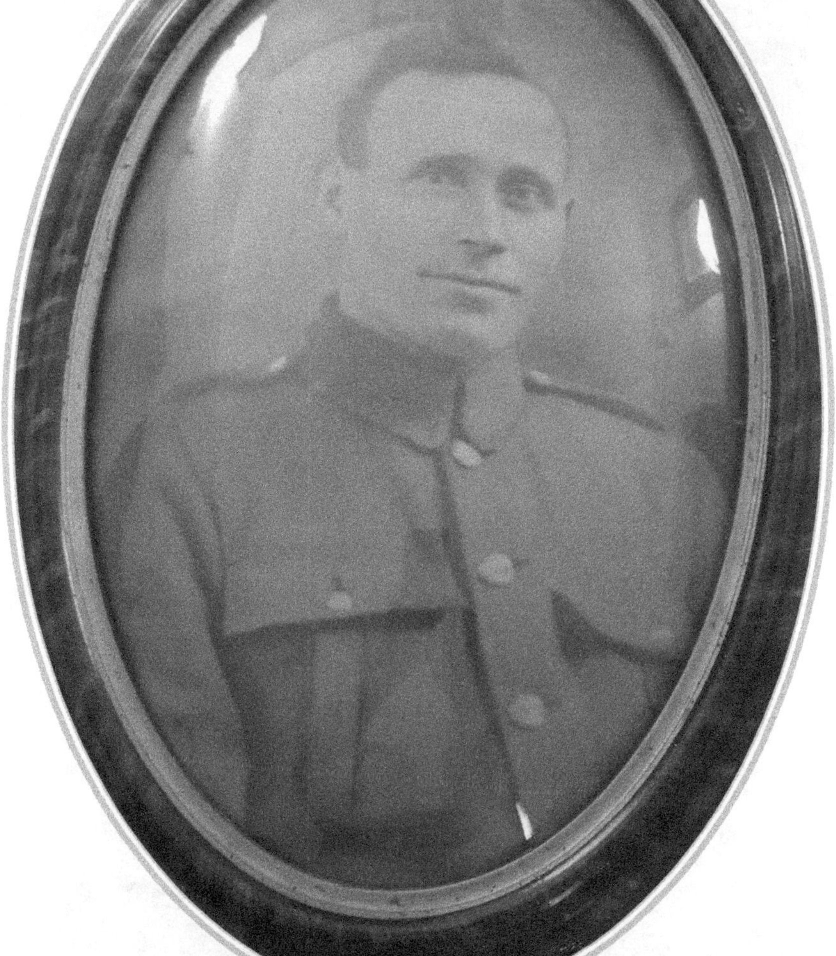

Father Samuel Butt in uniform -1917

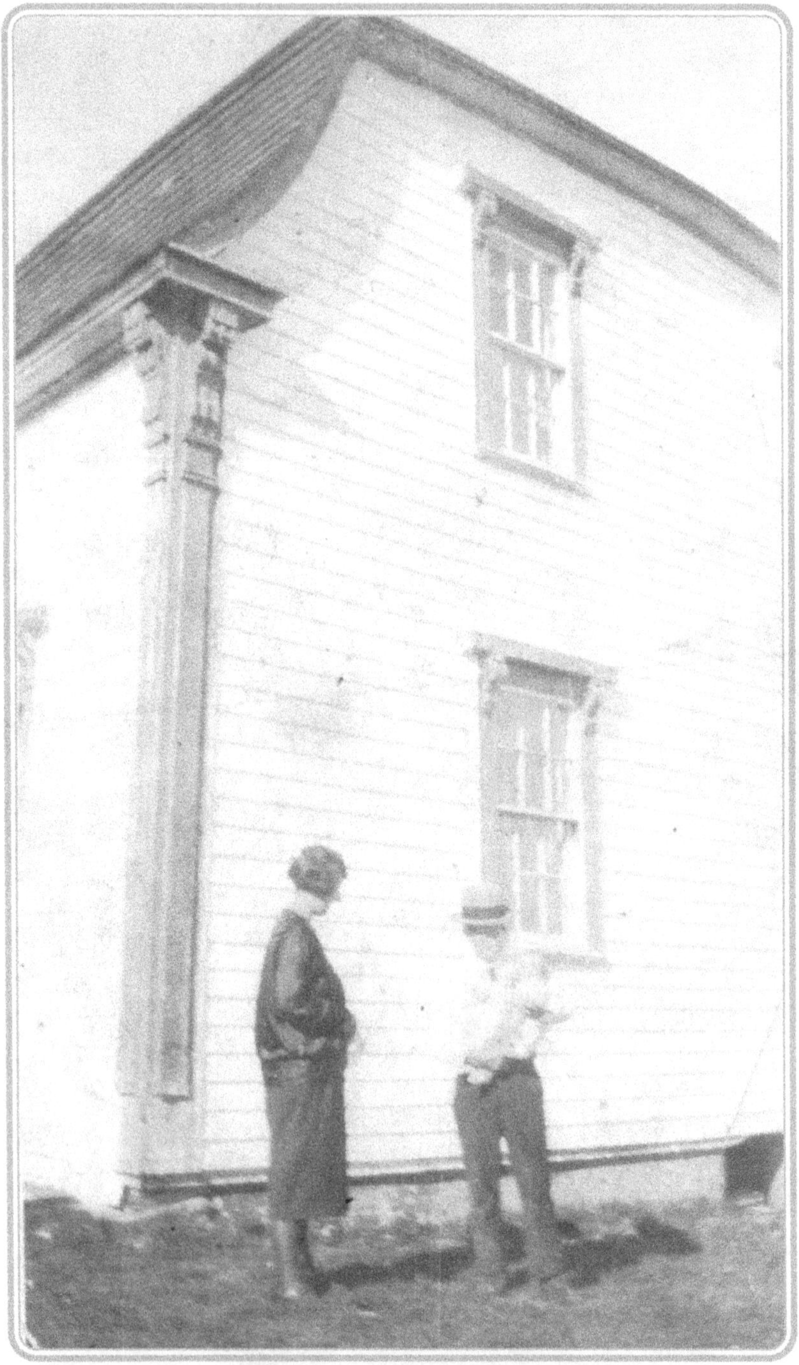

Cavell's christening 1927

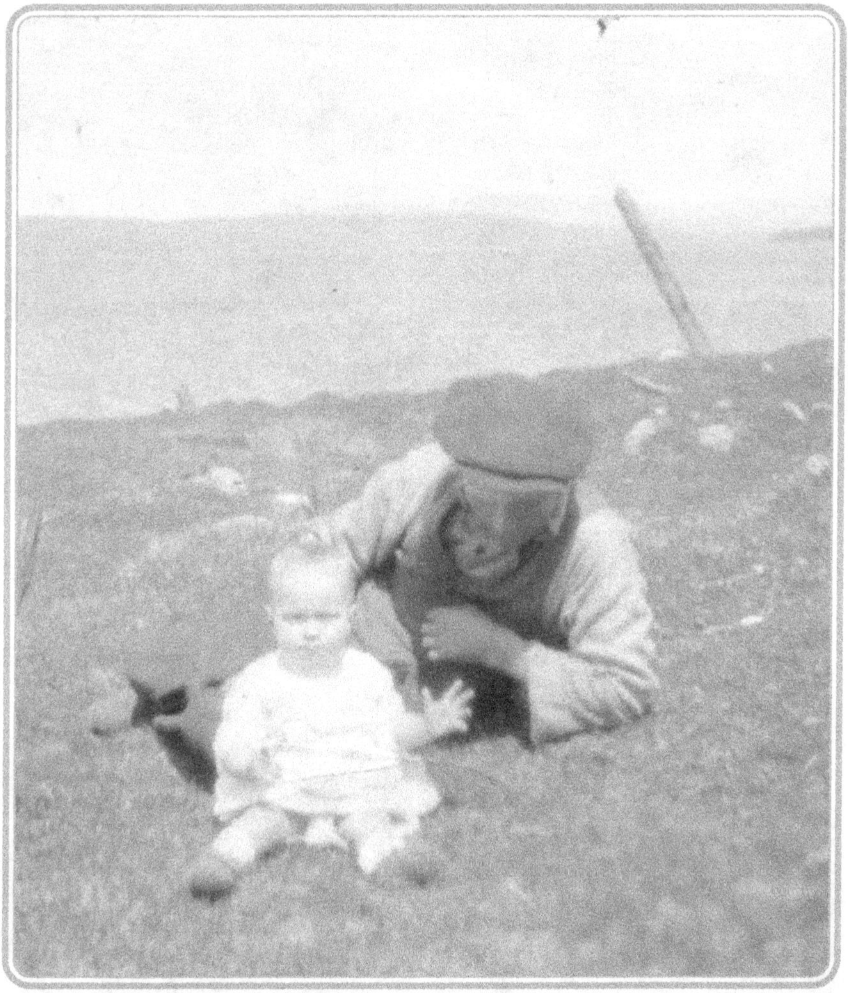

Dad and Cavell 1928

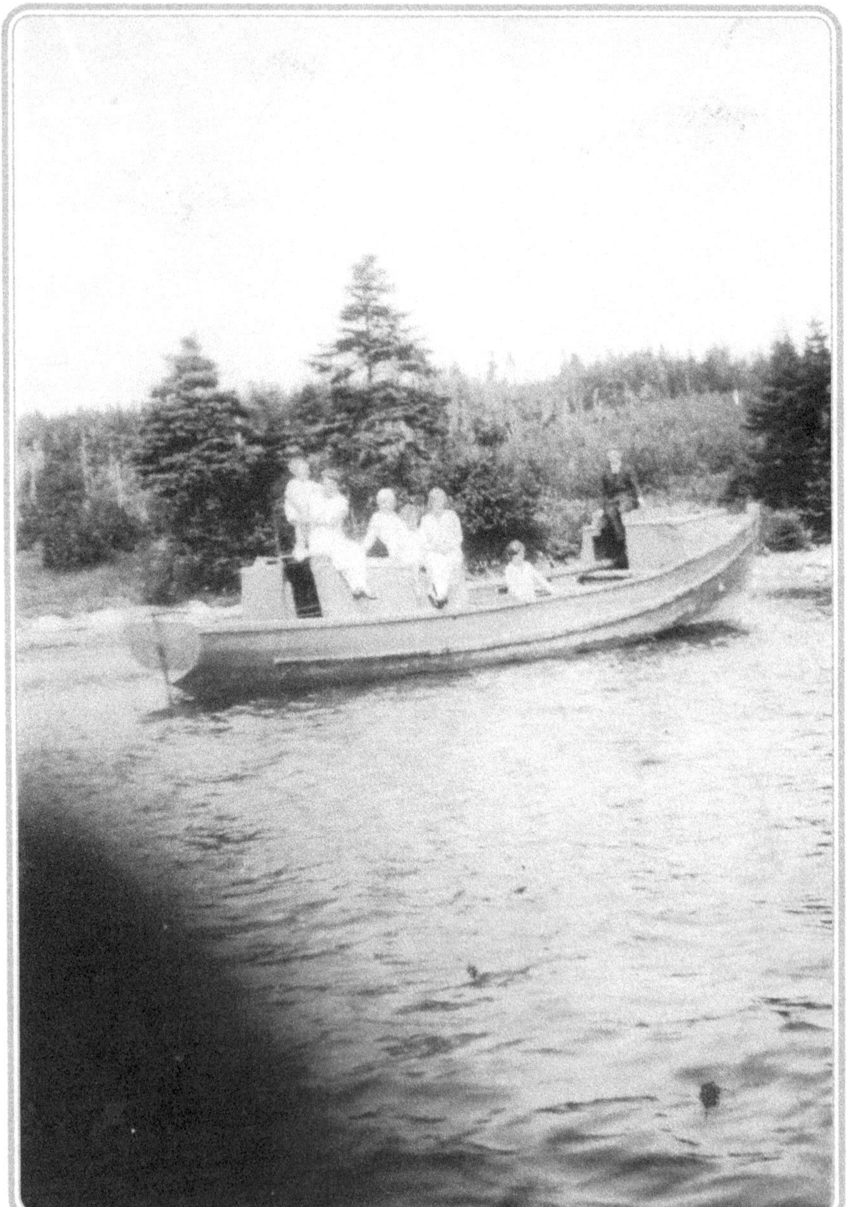

Picnic up St.George's river on our boat the 'Mayflower'

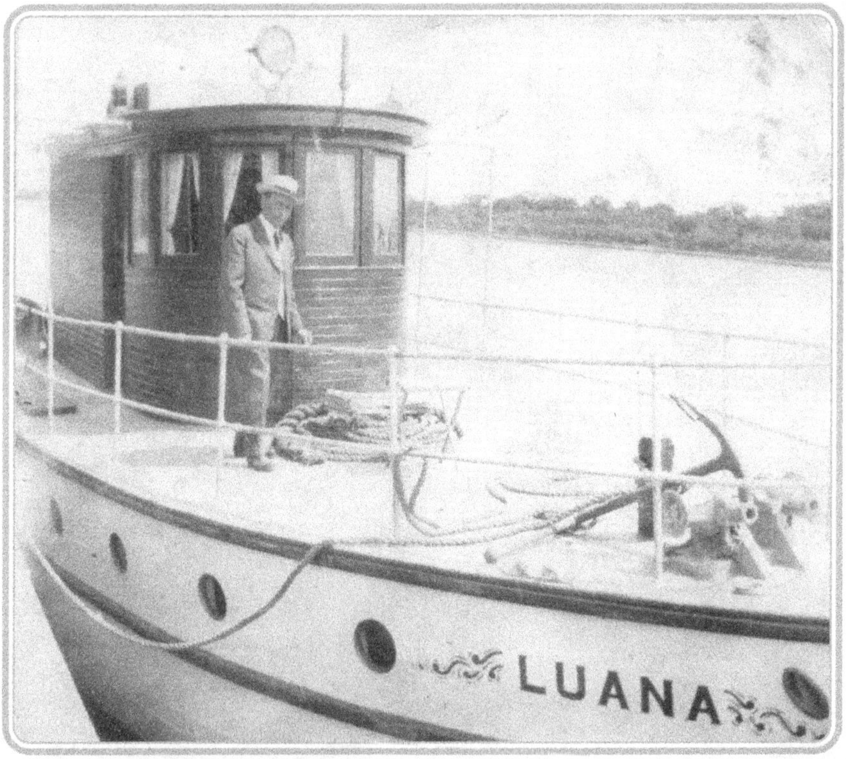

Dad on Lake Winnipeg as skipper of a private pleasure boat.

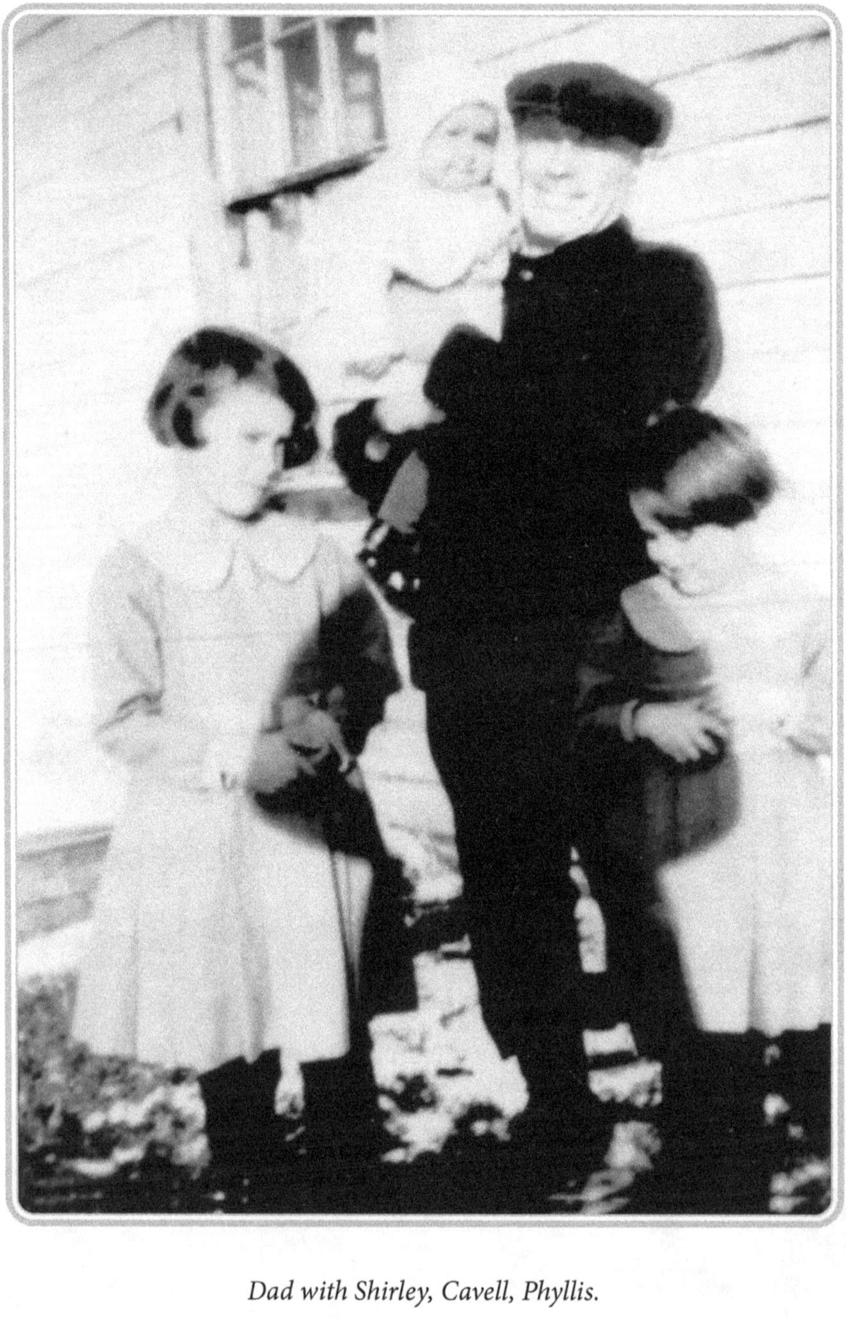

Dad with Shirley, Cavell, Phyllis.

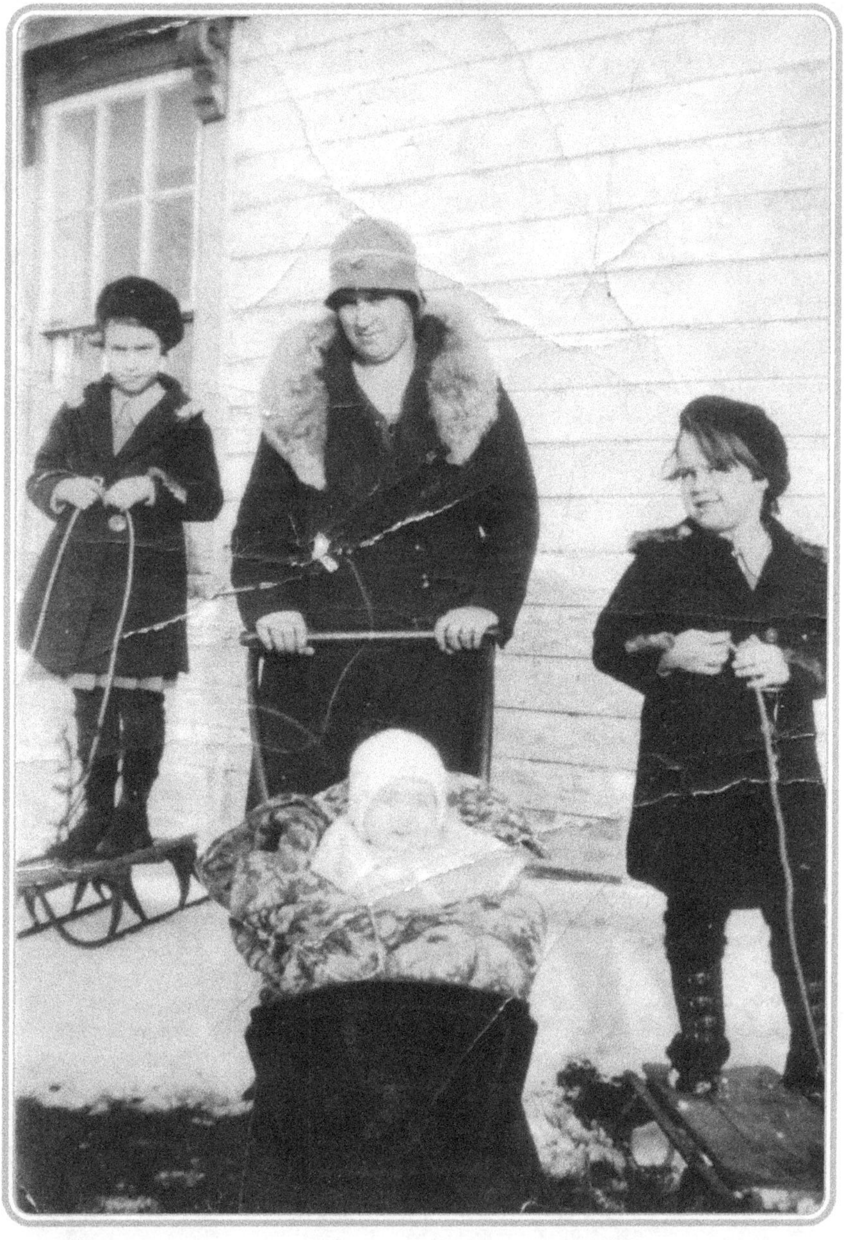

Mom and 3 girls - winter

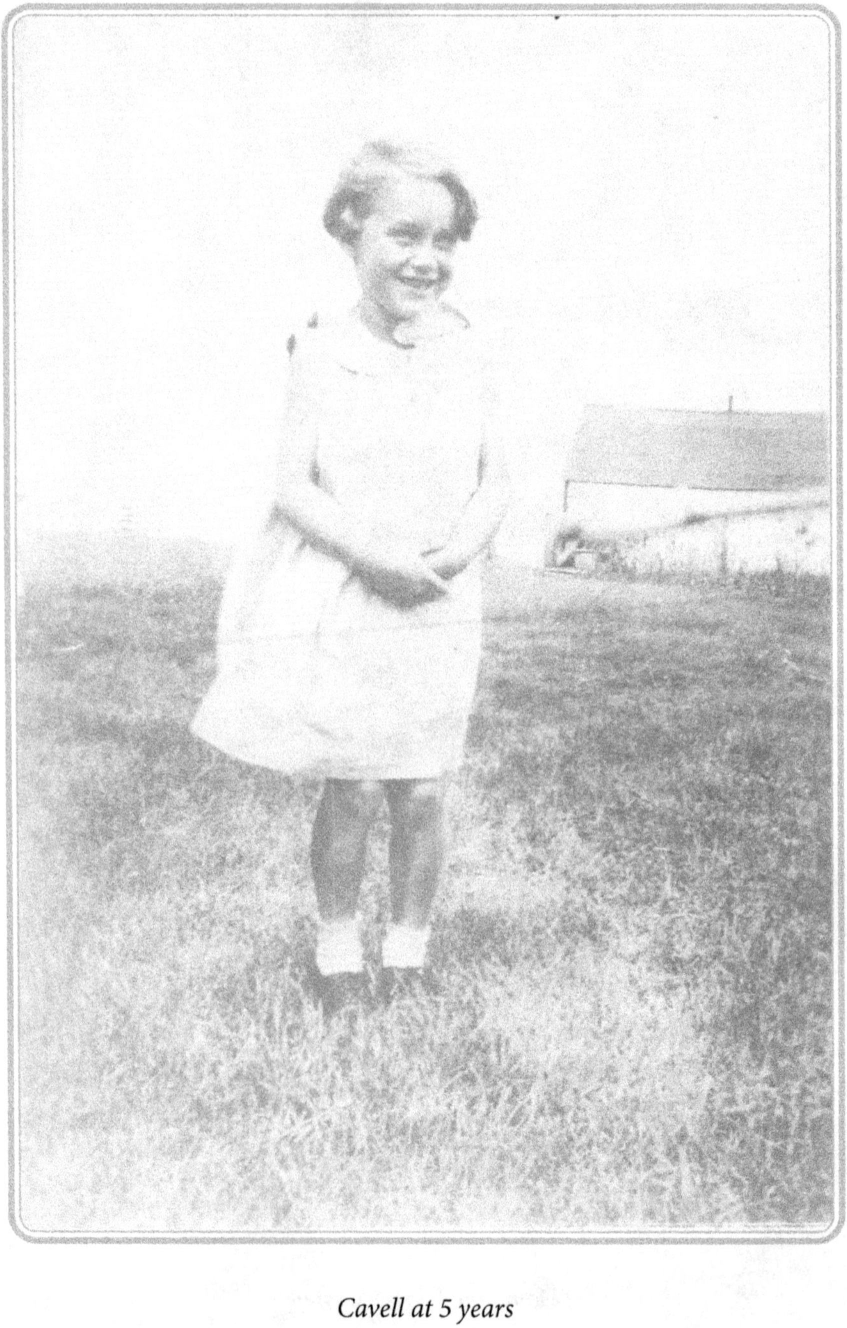

Cavell at 5 years

ANNOUNCING CAVELL WHOLE WHEAT CEREAL;
WHAT ABOUT YOUR BREAKFAST THE FIRST MEAL OF THE DAY.

CAVELL CEREAL contains Vitamins A B and G. Prominent authorities on children's diet say:—Vitamin B is our great protective food, because it combats nervousness, constipation and poor appetite. They also say milk eaten with cereal, builds better growth, because the growth value of milk is largely vitamin G, and vitamin G can best perform its task when eaten with a food that contains the vitamin B. CAVELL CEREAL is palatable, wholesome, delicious and nutritious, possessing a RARE NUTTY flavour in all its fullness, and the rest of the fourteen mineral elements essential to complete bodily nutrition.

During the Seige of Kut-El-Amara in Mesopotamia in the World War the garrison suffered greatly from a shortage of food, the British troops using white flour only, suffered to some extent from the dread disease called Beri-Beri. The native soldiers whose bread had in it some of the Wheat germ, remained free from this trouble. Give your children and others, FREELY EVERY DAY, the VITAMINS so found in CAVELL CEREAL.

The following recipes are tested and can be made with ease:

First: For Cavell Cereal Porridge: Mix Cereal with cold water to a thick paste, stir into boiling water constantly to avoid lumping, bring to a boil, and cook TWO minutes only, stirring all the time. Serve with maple syrup, sugar or molasses, you will then enjoy the full Medicinal value of Cavell Cereal. The more it is cooked the less laxitive. One pound of Cavell Cereal equals two and two-thirds cupful, and makes a cereal Breakfast for eight people.

Second: Cold Cereal: Just serve Cavell Cereal with milk, sugar and a shake of salt (without cooking) and its excellence will surprise you.

Third: For Cavell Bread: Use one third the quantity of Cavell Cereal to that of white flour, add salt, pinch of butter and small quantity of sugar, mix fairly soft and warm. For good breadmaking, the ingredients should be kneaded five minutes to each pound of flour, and packed away warm to rise in the usual way, knead over in the morning, and let rise before setting in the pans for baking, and you will have successful bread.

Fourth: Cavell Muffins: Recipie offered by Mrs. A. G. Bartlett, Corner Brook. One-third cup butter, half cup sugar, two tablespoonfuls molasses, two eggs, one cup milk, two cups flour, four teaspoons baking powder, half teaspoon salt, two and half cups Cavell Cereal, one cup raisins. First cream the butter, add sugar, cream thoroughly together. Beat eggs, add molasses and milk. Add to butter and sugar mixture. Add Cavell Cereal and raisins, then bake in well greased pans in hot oven, about 450 degrees F., reduce to 365 degrees after ten minutes.

Five: Cavell Sponge Cake (delicious): 2 tablespoonfuls butter, ½ cup sugar, 2 eggs separated, 1½ cups Cavell Cereal, 1½ cups flour, 3 teaspoonfuls baking powder, ½ teaspoon salt, 1 cup milk. Cream butter and sugar thoroughly, add yolks one by one, beat whites to a stiff froth, add this with Cavell Cereal, and sifted flour, baking powder and salt, and milk. Mix lightly till all is well mixed, pour into well greased pan and bake in moderate oven 30 minutes or until done. (Have pan on wire ring to brown evenly).

Sixth: Quick Cavell Cereal Biscuits: One rounded cup Cavell Cereal, 1 rounded cup flour, 1 small teaspoon salt, 1 level teaspoon soda. Mix 4 level tablespoonfuls shortening, 1 cup sour milk, 1 tablespoonful sugar. Stir the two mixtures together, and beat two minutes; drop in small lots on a well greased pan and brown in a moderate oven. (If sweet milk is used, add 2 teaspoonfuls baking powder instead of soda.)

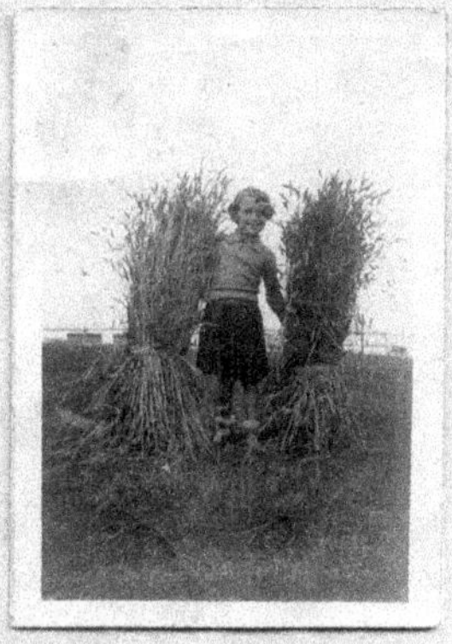

Seventh: Delicious Steamed or Boiled Pudding: I cup brown sugar (or molasses), 1 egg, 1 large tablespoonful shortening, 1 cup sour milk, 1 teaspoon soda, (or 2 teaspoonfuls baking powder and one cup sweet milk), 1 cup or more of raisins, nutmeg to flavour, 2 cups Cavell Cereal, 2 cups flour, Steam or boil one hour.

Let the experience of others be your guide, and follow the example of the following testimonals in choosing a Cereal for your Breakfast, that will start you off right on your day's work.

Mr. S. H. Butt, St. George's:—I have much pleasure in recommending your CAVELL CEREAL as a breakfast food. Personally I am very fond of it. (Signed) Yours truly, W. J. Milley, Curling.

Mr. S. H. Butt. Dear Sir:—I have personally used in my home your CAVELL CEREAL, and find it of excellent quality, and better than any imported cereal of the same grade. Yours truly, (signed) A. M. Dunphy, Curling.

Mr. S. H. Butt. Dear Sir:—We have used your CAVELL CEREAL in our home and find it excellent breakfast food, and highly recommend it for use in every home. Yours truly, (signed) Eugene Baggs, Curling.

Mr. S. H. Butt, St. George's. (Telegram from Hon. Frank Pike, Port aux Basques):—Have tried your Whole Wheat Cereal and find it appetizing and satisfying stop This Cereal makes an excellent base for a solid meal. (Signed) Frank Pike.

Mr. S. H. Butt. Dear Sir:—We used your CAVELL CEREAL to day, Oct. 1, 1934 for the first time, and our guests are highly satisfied with it as a breakfast food, and I take pleasure in endorsing your product as a high class Cereal. (Signed) A. F. Burns, Manager, Humber House, Corner Brook.

Mr. S. H. Butt, St. George's. Dear Sir:—CAVELL CEREAL I find to be an ideal breakfast food. It can be used in various ways to good advantage. (Signed) J. T. Clarke, (Rev.), Channel.

Mr. S. H. Butt, St. George's. Dear Mr. Butt:—We are using "CAVELL" Whole Wheat Cereal as one of our regular breakfast cereals, and take great pleasure in recommending it as an ideal breakfast food. "If you want to keep on the sunny side of life use 'Cavell Whole Wheat Cereal'." (Signed) J. T. Wharton, Manager, Glynmill Inn, Corner Brook.

If you want your grocer to sell it, please ask him to order today from the undersigned.

MANUFACTURED BY

S. H. BUTT

ST. GEORGE'S Newfoundland

PLEASE HANG ME UP

Western Star, Curling.

Dad's flyer for Cavell Whole Wheat Cereal.

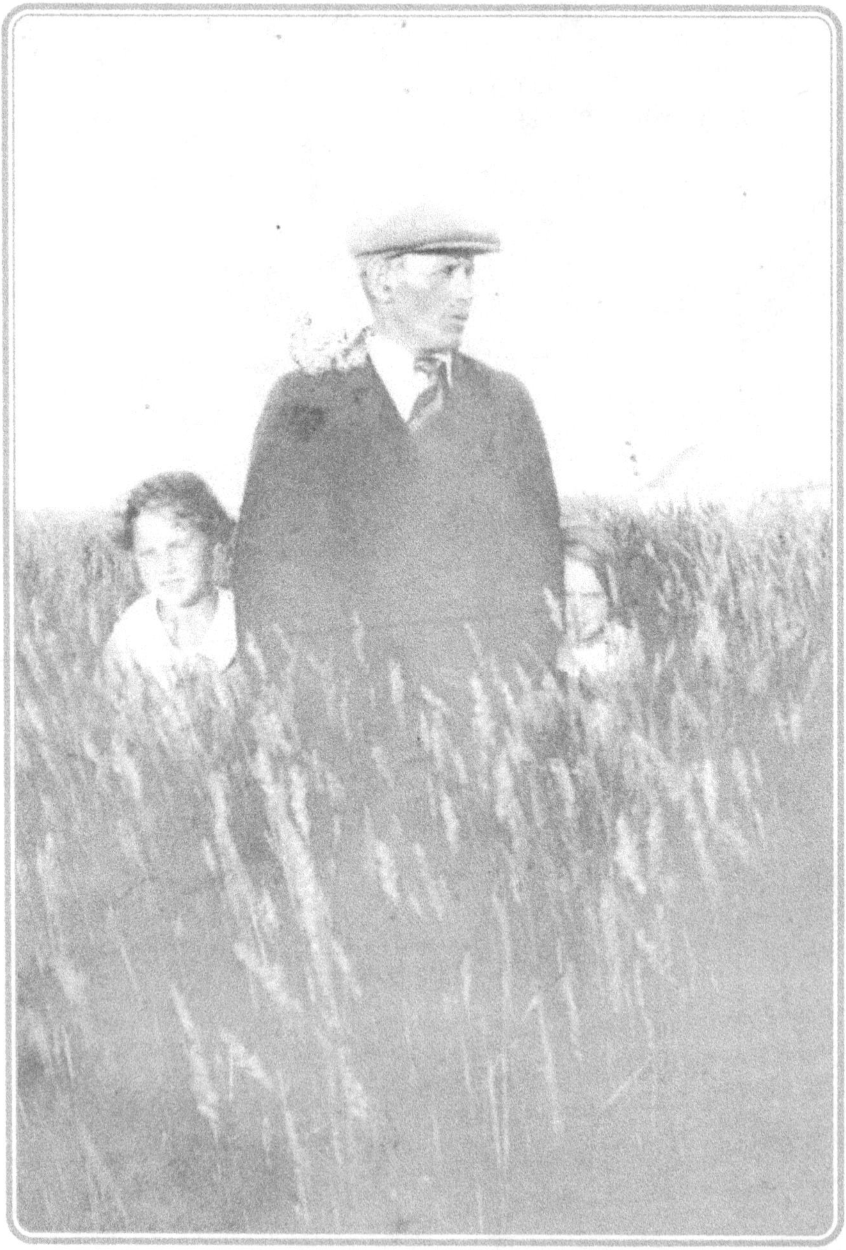

Dad, Phyllis, Cavell in St Georges wheat field

VISITING

When we didn't have Sunday School or it was over for the day, we went visiting and that was great fun. People made a fuss over us and offered us cake and tea. We must have made quite a sight, two grown-ups and three children turning in through people's gates unannounced, though this was customary before people had telephones. We were always warmly welcomed, for our parents were well-respected in the community and had many friends. The people I particularly remember were the Goodyears (not the teacher) whose daughter, Maudie, was a good friend of Mom's. She had had infantile paralysis (polio) and walked with a cane. Another was the Losse Pieroways whom we called Aunt and Uncle. They lived up the road near the church in a house that was the same design as ours. It is still there.

If there were families that had sickness or a new baby, we would stop in to drop off a treat or a gift but not make a visit of it. It was just nice to be out walking with our mom and dad. Roddy White, a retired monsignor from St. George's and a family friend, remembers us all walking along the road in the winter. Shirley rode in the special push sleigh on runners that Dad had made, and Phyllis and I walked beside it holding the handle.

One summer, for a while we visited an elderly man (who shall remain nameless) and his wife whom Dad employed in lobster season. We visited fairly frequently on Sunday afternoons in the summer, pushing Shirley in her carriage. His wife grew daisies around the front of the house, and we loved going there. Our visiting started when Dad arranged for the ship's surgeon from a visiting warship to see if anything could be done for the varicose ulcers on the old fellow's leg. The surgeon recommended treatment—an ointment spread on old cotton pieces scorched on the top of the stove to sterilize them. I was fascinated. For some time afterwards, we would go down there on Sunday afternoons to see how he was doing. Once when Phyllis and I were playing around outside, the old man came out and invited us into his work shed to see something. This sounded interesting! We followed him in, and he busied himself at his workbench with his back toward us. Then he turned around holding his huge, erect penis in his hand! We were flabbergasted; the first thing I thought of was it must be sore like his red and swollen leg. He wanted us to touch it, but we shook our heads and left.

I was confused. We were taught to respect our elders and do what they said, but this didn't seem right! I had never seen anything like that before. We were very private about our private parts in our house, and for someone to deliberately show us his seemed shameful. Even to speak of it to our parents was too embarrassing to contemplate, so we didn't. We sensed that this was something that would upset them, and we didn't want to do that. So, in a way we were protecting our parents from knowing about his shameful behaviour. We told only Audrey, who thought we were making it all up.

Going down to see Aunt Mary at their farm at Black Bank was exciting. Either this was spontaneous or our parents didn't tell us about it in advance to spare themselves the commotion when we became excited. Of course it meant a boat trip, which we loved. Our boat was our only vehicle and took us many places. My favourite spot on the boat was up in the bow watching the water fly up on either side of the boat with my hair flying straight out behind me. Nothing could beat it!

Once, on our way to Aunt Mary's in the motor boat, Dad spotted something in the water and went over to investigate. It was the top of a wooden mast with ropes and hardware still on it, and he insisted on towing it to shore. It was HEAVY and the boat at full power could hardly move. Mom was sure that the load would tip us over and begged Dad to let it go, but at last we made it to shore at Barachois Brook. Everything that was salvageable was shared between my dad and his peers. There was a use for everything. I was more worried that there was a sunken boat on the other end of the mast!

The farm at Black Bank was mostly pasture backed by low trees in the distance as far as I could see, and horses grazed in the field. There was a big barn, too, and black flies by the millions! We weren't used to them at our place, and as the number of bites grew, the more we scratched. We wore scarves around our heads, but they didn't help much. However, the visit meant a meal at someone else's house where we were welcome, and that was exciting. There was also a telephone on the wall. This was new to us and we listened in amazement to the different combinations of long rings and short ones that allowed people to hear each other through the wires!

The trip home in the evening was cooler but beautiful. The evening skies in St. George's Bay were indescribable. The colours filled the whole sky with reds, oranges and turquoises that continued long after the sun dropped into the sea.

One time, Dad took Mary Alexander, a family friend, to see her dying father who lived in Port au Port. Dad took the whole family with him for the long trip over Bay St. George, the farthest I had ever been on the water. It was a beautiful afternoon and the trip was wonderful. Our friend was worried about her father who had a kidney condition and whose arms and legs were extremely swollen. Children were included in all family activities, so I went in with Dad to see this sick man. My father was so warm and compassionate to him and spoke to him in a language I couldn't understand. Dad explained later that the man spoke only French, a language I had never heard before. It was the only time I ever heard Dad speak it.

The part of Newfoundland where the man lived was called Port au Port, a wishbone-shaped peninsula jutting out into the Gulf of St. Lawrence, the south shore of which helped form Bay St. George. The settlers were mostly French speaking people whose ancestors fled from Acadia (now New Brunswick) after the British—who were defeated in the American Revolution—moved north to the territories they still held. Worried that these French speaking pacifists would not be loyal, the British deported them to the other French speaking part of North America: Louisiana. Many families came to this area to escape deportation, and their descendants, who are still there, can trace their ancestry back to that time.

Other French settlers there were the deserters from fishing vessels from France hoping for a less arduous life ashore. One teenager, named Peter LeRoux, deserted and found refuge in Grandpa Nathaniel's house in St. George's. The story goes that when the French search party came looking for him, Grandpa hid him, and Peter remained a family friend. As a young child I remember him vividly, probably because his English didn't sound like ours. On one of his visits when I was a child, I received a smack on the bottom from him in response to something I said (probably regarding his accent!). He married a local girl and raised a family, one of whom has returned from abroad to live in the old family home.

On the way home from Port au Port, the sun was setting, and Mom told me to watch the big red sun drop into the ocean, which I thought peculiar. She explained it was actually the earth turning and if I watched I would see how fast it turned! Why the water didn't just fall off the earth was explained by gravity, and it was hard to understand how fast the earth would have to spin to achieve that. My mom said we already had the answer: a day and a night when the sun came up again! I remember thinking what a beautiful, wonderful world we lived in. It was amazing to me to watch this process as the sky turned red, orange, turquoise and peach. I have never forgotten it.

One of our adventures on the water nearly turned into a tragedy. Before we ventured out in the boat, Dad would read the sky for signs of what the weather was going to be. He was usually pretty accurate, but one time he either misjudged or there was no sign of what was coming. There were no weather predictions in the paper and anyhow the *Western Star* came only once a week. We also received the *Family Herald* and *Weekly Star* from Montreal, but there was nothing useful in it as far as weather was concerned. Few people had radios and we didn't own one. Dad had a Farmer's Almanac that he frequently consulted for moon phases and tide times.

One Sunday in the summer, Mom and Dad were planning a trip to Heatherton a few miles down the coast to see Great-uncle George Butt and his wife, Aunt Letetia, who wasn't well. We put out and soon rounded Sandy Point. We were in the open Gulf of St. Lawrence where the waves, travelling for hundreds of miles, were bigger than anything in St. George's Harbour. As we travelled down the coast the wind picked up and soon the waves were tossing us around. There was nowhere to put in as by now we were running along a section of the coast where the cliffs towered fifty or sixty feet above us with no break and nowhere to get out of the storm.

Phyllis and I were sent into the "cuddy," the little decked-over space at the front of the boat where there was some canvas and old clothes to lie on. By then the boat was almost standing on its end. Mom later said that every time the boat went down into a trough, she was lifted off her seat, the wave broke over it and the next instant she sat back down on a seat running with water. But she stayed outside with Dad, both to keep him company and to bail. He was fighting to keep the boat pointed into the wind, for to let the waves hit us sideways would have swamped the boat and thrown us into the sea. I kept wanting to come outside to see what was going on, for Phyllis and I were really scared. I was sure the boat was going to sink but Mom kept telling us that Dad was in control of the boat and everything was going to be all right. I had to believe her.

After what seemed like a very long time, we could see the break in the cliffs that the fishermen of Heatherton used, and we knew we were safely there. Aunt Mary told us later that she had been scanning the water with her binoculars when she saw us clear Sandy Point. When the storm came up she had doubts we would make it. Only Dad's seamanship and a good deal of praying got us through.

PICNICS

Some Sundays, the only day Dad didn't work, we would have a picnic. Sometimes it would be up at the big hill, which was a wooded property that we owned across the highroad. We loved going up there, first through a meadow and then into a clearing at the top of the hill where we would spread the picnic things. Phyllis and I thought it pretty wild up there and hoped to see rabbits, but all we found were blueberries. That was bounty enough as we adored blueberries.

Another favourite spot for a picnic was outside the fence on the bank, but it was more likely to be in the field between the house and the bank. I loved picnics and still do. I can't remember what we ate, but the food didn't matter. The main thing was that we were eating outside—pretty exotic!

One picnic that stands out in my mind was on the back of Sandy Point. Dad had come home in the middle of the morning announcing that he had to go out on some business, and would we like to go! Mom was in the middle of the Monday morning washing and she looked for a minute at the nice warm water that she had heated on the stove. To leave it would have meant wasting the water brought from the well by the pail full, heating more and starting all over again. But she didn't hesitate long. In no time we were on our way down to the wharf with a few supplies for lunch, and we were away!

We headed out toward the tip of Sandy Point, rounded it and turned left to go down the coast. I don't know the reason for the trip that day but soon we saw a fisherman in the distance hauling his nets, and we headed his way. He was pulling in salmon and before we knew it Dad had bought one for lunch. I remember Mom wondering what they could cook it in when one of them hit on the bright idea of using an old pail that Dad carried in the boat. He scoured it with sand, filled it with sea water, lit a fire and put in chunks of the fresh salmon. Soon we were feasting on salmon fresh from the sea; I have never eaten a more delicious meal. Of course, we had to have tea. No outing in Newfoundland is complete without boiling the kettle and having a "mug-up."

Dad's birthday was on August 15, and we always had a special picnic on that day. The weather was usually fine for travelling longer distances on the water, and that day was reserved for a trip up Main River (St. George's River). On one birthday picnic up there, to her surprise Mom discovered a large patch of ripe raspberries! This was a rare treasure, and nothing would do but that we all pick raspberries until the patch was cleaned. She was able to make many bottles of raspberry jam for the winter. We had happy memories of that afternoon picking berries in spite of hordes of mosquitoes!

We had to gauge the time of our return by the tide, and picking the precious raspberries had made it a concern. On the way home where the river met the sea, we had to pass under the railway trestle that spanned the river's mouth near Stephenville Crossing. At low tide there was no problem with headroom, but it was a different story if the tide were in. Dad was concerned about whether we would have room to go under the trestle. I was in my favourite place with the wind in my face at the bow of the boat in my red coat that Mom had made for me. We were approaching fast and there certainly wasn't much room to spare. The boat was going as fast as Dad could drive it, and it became a race between us and the tide, which was pouring up the river. At the last minute as we came up to the trestle, he yelled for everybody to duck their heads. We skimmed under with only inches to spare!

OUR LIVE-IN FRIENDS

On occasion we kept boarders. When I was seven or so, the new minister, Rev. AN Holmes, and his family stayed with us for what seemed like the whole summer while the parsonage was prepared. They had a little boy named Douglas, around a year and a half old, whom Phyllis and I would wheel around in his carriage. We really liked the Holmes'. There was a lovely warm quality to them, and they became good family friends. It fell to Mr. Holmes a couple of years later to bury my father, which must have been hard for him. During the time between Dad's death and our leaving St. George's, he visited many times, and each time Shirley would climb into his lap and stay there. It seemed that she missed her dad and a male presence because she never did that to female visitors.

Bob Milley was our favourite boarder. One day he appeared at our door asking if Mom would consider boarding him. He was being transferred to St. George's by the Bank of Montreal and needed a place to stay. I guess Mr. Wornell, the bank manager who knew us, suggested he try us. Mr. Milley was with us most of two years, I think, and when he left I mourned his loss like a member of our family.

I also missed his candies! I don't know if he kept candies in his room all the time but one summer he had what looked like a huge tin of brightly wrapped candies in there. Of course, we were offered some when they arrived and thereafter they were a tremendous temptation for me! I knew where he kept them on his dresser in his room and eventually he realized they were going down, so he spoke to my mother. I hated to admit I was the one who helped them disappear! It was a great loss to me, and I was told not to take things that did not belong to me!

It was Bob Milley who gave Phyllis and me our first car ride. Bob was "going with" Regina MacLennan, whose father had a car, and as a special treat he was lending it to Bob to go on an outing. It was decided that we should go to Black Bank to see Aunt Mary. As we were heading down the grade that approached the bridge over Barachois Brook, the car gained speed and Bob applied the brakes. The light covering of snow was enough to put the car into a skid. To me it was all part of the excitement, but I soon felt the terror in the car as we neared the open water spanned only by a narrow wooden bridge with no sides! We made it safely over, but everyone was shaken. The tide was running and the water there was deep and black—we wouldn't have had a chance! On the way back we could see that we had come within inches of the edge. We were certainly being looked after that day!

In Grade 1 I had trouble with arithmetic. Because Mr. Milley was a banker, my parents thought perhaps he could help me at this difficult time of my life! One day he came upon Mom and me in the kitchen working on my homework, and it was not going well. I was not getting it, Mom was losing her patience, and I was in tears. I hated anyone to see me cry and to make matters worse, Mr. Milley crouched behind Mom's back and made faces at me! How could one laugh and cry at the same time? Smiles won out and he took over the lesson. My memory of the outcome has faded!

Harold Morris, our cousin, lived with us for a year when I was five or six. When Aunt Ruth Morris and her family moved to Toronto she asked her two siblings, Aunt Mary and my dad, if they would take two of her eight children for a year until they could become established in Toronto. Alice went to live with Aunt Mary on their farm at Black Bank where she would have a big sister, Ruth, and Harold came to us. He was a big brother to Phyllis and me. With no son, Dad became quite attached to him and asked his parents if he could remain with us, but his family wanted him back with them, so he had to leave much to our regret. I felt the loss keenly and moped around for days.

In the meantime, Harold's family had to deal with a tragedy. My Aunt Ruth was a strong person, but this incident must have tested her limits. When she arrived in Canada with her six children, immigration authorities wanted to know about her artificial leg. It had been amputated years before after a road accident, but the authorities put it down to TB of the bone, which wasn't uncommon at that time. In spite of Aunt Ruth's assertions that it had been only a severe compound fracture, the family was needlessly put into quarantine for weeks. While there, the baby contracted diphtheria and died. What strength it must have taken to deal with that!

Mr. Bursey, a new minister, also lived with us for a time. He did not smile much and kept to himself. He was a tall, thin young man, given to few words and likely not long out of college when he came to St. George's. Being on the board of the church, I'm sure Dad knew of his need of accommodation and because we had a big house with lots of room, he invited him to our place. We called his room "the study" and that is where he stayed except for mealtime, choosing not to socialize.

There is a story regarding Rev. Bursey and my father's commitment to his faith. Mr. Bursey's room was upstairs with a window looking out to sea and had its own little stove, which in the summer gradually filled with chocolate bar wrappers. As chocolate bars were a rarity in our house, Phyllis and I became envious, but no treats were offered. One day at suppertime, he suddenly pushed back his chair saying, "I can no longer exist on the food in this house." The table became very silent, my dad at one end and Mr. Bursey at the other with me sitting next to him. Dad said very evenly that nutritious food (nutrition was big with him) was being served in this house and if Mr. Bursey felt that way he was free to move. I can't remember the exchange except for the above comments, which included this last one: "Don't think this will keep me from church for I will continue to worship there supposing the Devil himself were in the pulpit!" Mr. Bursey left the table, went upstairs, packed and very quickly went out the door. We watched him walk up through the field to the road.

Mom and Dad thought it had been pre-arranged for he went directly to Mr. and Mrs. Goodyear's where there were two young people close to his own age. He obviously wanted to move to his friends' house but didn't know how to do it. On Sunday we were in our pew two rows from the front while Mr. Bursey preached. I don't remember his text!

HOME COOKING

On the whole we were a pretty healthy family. Our diet was simple: vegetables we grew ourselves and fresh fish of all descriptions—cod, herring, mackerel, salmon, scallops, lobster and a tuna steak once in awhile. Nobody ate tuna, it was a nuisance fish called horse mackerel that tore up fishermen's nets. We had loads of milk, cream and butter from our cow. Fresh meat was rare, and we had it only when we killed an animal or bought a roast of moose from someone. We didn't kill a chicken too often as we depended on their eggs, and even then it was an older hen whose laying had slowed down. Though old, their flavour was the best, especially with the stuffing flavoured with savoury from the kitchen garden.

The rest of the time the meat was salt beef packed in barrels of brine in Toronto. It was a traditional food and we loved it cooked with turnip, cabbage, potatoes and sometimes pease pudding. This consists of split peas cooked in a bag in the same pot as the dinner, then mashed with butter! I still cook pease pudding with my salt beef dinner when my sons are coming over, though the bag is almost worn out! In Newfoundland one can still buy pudding bags in most grocery stores.

Also frequently cooked along with the dinner was the "duff." This was a batter boiled in a bag and flavoured with raisins, allspice and molasses. Our family loved it as dessert, but some old timers ate it at dinner with "pot liquor" (the vegetable and meat water the dinner was cooked in).

VARIOUS "CURES"

Occasionally, we developed colds and then we had to endure "the cure." My mother was particularly worried about my chest colds as I had contracted whooping cough as a six month old and had almost died. This is an infection that is characterized by violent spasms of coughing that end in a "whoop" when one's air is exhausted and leaves the sufferer limp. Mom told me once that she would often go into the bedroom to check me in my cradle not knowing whether she would find me alive or dead.

With this in my background, I got the works! Mom made a chest covering of a woolen cloth that had a front and back and was put on after a generous portion of goose grease had been rubbed on my chest. It itched like crazy under the wool and I begged her not to put it on but to no avail. I suppose all that itching must have brought blood to the area enhancing the action of the goose grease, which many people swore by and was available from a neighbour. I guess she was worried enough to try anything in those days before antibiotics.

Another concoction Mom used was a few drops of Friar's Balsam on a spoonful of sugar with Carnation tinned milk to top it off. It tasted good because it was sweet and *that* I didn't mind!

Mother also made her own cough candies. We often made molasses pull taffy in our house and when we had a cold she added a few drops of kerosene and black pepper! The taste wasn't great but call it candy and kids will eat anything!

Dad had his own way of dealing with a cold. He went to bed in his pure wool Stanfield's long underwear, piled on extra blankets, and covered his head with the bedding so that the air was moist. He stayed there, drinking water and sweating, while Mom changed the sheets frequently. At the end of two days he got up feeling much better. Phyllis and I would look at him and wonder how anyone could keep their head covered that long and survive!

I got into trouble at school for spitting in my desk drawer! This sounds really weird but at the time it made sense to me. I was probably around seven or eight and had been bothered for a long time—it felt like all year—by a condition that was known as "catarrh." As far as I can tell it was a chronic infection of the sinuses with lots of postnasal drip. The doctor advised that I sniff up salty water into my nose, which would have the effect of draining the sinuses and irrigating the nasal passage. Unfortunately, he suggested that the salty water could be sea water. Well! I didn't have that much trouble with the sniffing part, but the sea water STUNG! But my mom had to follow doctor's orders and the stuff wasn't diluted. I put up such a fuss that my mother gave up eventually, but the drip didn't. Because we used cloth handkerchiefs, I didn't want to spit that revolting stuff into my handkerchief for my mother to wash. So, I took to spitting in my drawer instead.

One day Mr. Goodyear caught me and came to my desk to see what was going on. He took one look in my drawer and wished he hadn't! He was disgusted, took away the drawer and sent a note home. I did without the drawer till the end of the year. I don't remember any repercussions at home; my parents were probably embarrassed too. I was given something burnable to spit into and I don't know who cleaned up the drawer. I've included this story because I've been embarrassed about it all my life and finally I can let it go! That's progress!

ADULT TIME OUT 1

My parents hardly ever went out without us, and to go out for an evening by themselves was unheard of. Moreover, we would have seen ourselves as deprived; after all, visiting was a highlight for us. One winter evening when everything was frozen solid, they told us they were going skating. This was very big news as they had never before gone out in the evening. Besides, Phyllis and I had always done our skating in the daylight when we could see! Not only that, a stranger was coming to our house when our parents weren't home! Mrs. Garland, a neighbour, came to stay with us. I don't think she had ever been in our house before though we knew her to see her, and Mr. Garland often brought us a load of firewood by horse and sleigh.

Shirley was already in her crib, but the minute the door closed on our parents she started to cry. And she cried and cried and cried—ear piercing screams. She was really angry, and nothing would comfort her. Phyllis and I pulled out all the tricks we knew that usually worked but not tonight! We were getting pretty upset when Mrs. Garland finally came up with a trick of her own. She found a small square of cotton, put a teaspoon of sugar on it, tied it around with a string and stuck it in Shirley's mouth. It worked! She explained it was something people would do in earlier days. She called it a "sugar tit"!!

Dad worked every day but Sunday. Six-day weeks were the norm. Taking holidays away from work was unusual in our world where people had to tend to their nets and animals constantly. One time I overheard Mom saying to Dad that there were places where men actually were taking time off. I can't remember the outcome of that conversation, but it could have planted a seed for later on when they both went to Corner Brook for a few days. This was before Shirley was born. When they returned, Mom told us about going to see a moving picture where the pictures actually moved and people on the screen talked. It seemed unbelievable to us and it was only many years later that we saw our first movie. She told us that in this movie a little girl sang and danced. Her name was Shirley Temple. The next spring on April 22, 1934, my sister Shirley was born, the first Shirley in St. George's.

Dad and Mom had friends in Corner Brook called the Bartletts. We all descended upon them to see the celebration of King George V's twenty-five years on the throne in 1935. It seemed to be a big deal! That year all the school children were given a silver medal commemorating the event. Bob Milley was boarding with us by then and we all went into Corner Brook to see the big parade—the first parade I had ever seen. Lots of people were marching, there were more cars than I had ever seen, and there was a band that I thought was much too loud. Bob Milley was from there and he seemed pretty excited to run along pacing the parade with his collie named Laddie. There was certainly a lot of excitement, and I began to long for the peace and quiet of St. George's. I don't know what happened to my medal!

OUR FAMILY GROWS

A few months later, I noticed my mother had gained weight and one day while she was ironing, I said as much. She wasn't prepared for my keen observation and certainly didn't view it as an opportunity to tell me she was pregnant! She simply denied it even though she had become very large when viewed from the side! She was a woman of her times; children weren't told the facts of life when they asked questions. It wasn't until I was ten or so that my cousin, Bob Vardy, filled me in on the details. He lived in St. John's and he and his friend had spent some time devouring that particular section of *The Books of Knowledge* that many families owned!

The Sunday she went into labour with Shirley, our mother didn't get up for breakfast. She said she was tired, but she was often tired and didn't stay in bed! But who was I to question? I got on with helping Dad get breakfast. We were told that Phyllis and I were going to visit Dad's cousin, Norman Butt, and his wife, Floss, for a while. This was unusual because our visits to that family were brief and only with Mom there. However, we walked up through the field and after a few quiet words spoken on the side to Floss, Dad left us there.

It seemed like a very long time before he came back for us with the biggest smile that I had ever seen on his face. He announced there was a new baby sister waiting for us at home. What an enormous thing to have happened in our family, but why didn't we know she was coming? We were always told of other visitors' expected arrival! After all, this was more exciting than any ordinary visitor, even more exciting than Christmas!

Anyway, we got on our coats and walked with him down through the field to see this baby. Any babies I had seen were cute little things that I loved to play with, but the one that had landed in our house was a mess! She had a fat, red face and let out the most bloodcurdling screams. And we were supposed to kiss this thing and love her?! That was asking a lot as things stood, and after a few minutes of this screaming, I was glad to get out of the room.

There seemed to be a mystery connected to all this. Where had she come from? The train brought parcels and people and there had been no trains that day; even the post office was closed! They told us the stork had brought the baby, but what was a stork? No storks around St. George's that I had noticed! So, I felt that they weren't telling me what I needed to know, which didn't seem fair. In no time I had forgotten about the mystery because my parents always told the truth just as they insisted that I do, and I just had to accept what they were saying.

Besides, before long Shirley turned into a cute little baby who was fun to play with, which helped. Shirley had beautiful thick golden curls later on and Mother took a lot of time trying to make her unruly curly hair presentable. Without the sausage curls that Mom wound around her finger, Shirley's hair would look like "a birch broom in the fits" as an old Newfoundland saying went!

One day when Shirley had finished her dinner, she ran outside to play as usual, but things remained very quiet—too quiet! When Mom went to check, she found this toddler up to her elbows in the tar pot left by Dad after tarring the roof. Tar was all over her clothes, a big puddle on the bridge (deck), and all over her tangled golden curls! I can't remember what was said, but I remember Mom's dismay as she stripped Shirley down and wiped at the mess with kerosene, the old standby. I think Dad must have disappeared to the factory as I don't remember him being part of this scene!

There is another roof story that I remember. Every year the roof had to be inspected and the cracks filled with tar. Our house had high ceilings and a mansard roof, which meant the actual top was up almost to a three-story level. Dad had a big old wooden ladder with widely-spaced rungs that were a challenge for even his legs to span. One day as he was up on the roof, he suddenly heard a little voice say "Hello, Daddy." When he looked up, there was Phyllis' two-year-old face peeking over the edge of the roof. He almost fainted! He remained cool and said, "You stay right there until Daddy comes to get you." He managed to get her off the ladder safely and was then faced with another challenge: how to get them both twenty feet or so down the difficult ladder. He only had one hand for them both, but somehow he made it. I can still see him coming into the kitchen with Phyllis on one arm and falling into a chair. His face was drenched in perspiration. Phyllis probably thought it had been a great adventure! She was known for her adventurous spirit right to the end of her life!

THE RUNNING WATER EVENT!

The year before Shirley was born, Dad put plumbing in our house. It seemed to take forever but gradually the network of pipes grew. The wood-stove got a heater coil, which he connected to a water tank in the corner next to the stove near the hall door. We were warned to be careful for it could be hot. As I remember, it wasn't wrapped to conserve the heat, so it probably never got that hot! Pipes ran along the kitchen ceiling to the pantry at the end of the kitchen where a sink and faucets were installed. More pipes ran to the porch where Mom did the washing and two tubs appeared there, which Dad fitted with covers, so they became a sort of counter.

The pièce de résistance was the bathroom, a small room over the kitchen that he fitted with a bathtub; the water tank hung from the ceiling. What luxury! We could now take a bath and get wet all over instead of washing all over from a washbasin! What made this all the more miraculous was that Dad was not a plumber and had never done anything like this before. Actually, he didn't know there were things he couldn't do; he just studied the problem then worked on it.

To heat the bathroom, Dad cut a hole in the kitchen ceiling so the heat went up. One day he was taking a bath and we could see movement back and forth up there. I don't know whose idea it was, but Phyllis and I took up stations below the hole and took turns looking up to see what we could see. Fortunately for us Dad settled on a spot directly over the hole to dry himself. For the first time, Phyllis and I saw adult male genitalia! This was indeed something worth waiting for as in our house nobody showed their unclothed bodies. That was just taboo! Unfortunately for us, he happened to glance down and saw a pair of eyes—Phyllis'—looking up. He made us move and we didn't need any coaxing for we knew we were in trouble, or Phyllis was! He came downstairs with a purposeful step and went for the strap! Phyllis started crying and saying that Cavell had been peeking too. I denied it to save my hide and Phyllis got the licking! I didn't feel good about lying, but I didn't want the strap either. I had already tasted it once before and I lied to escape it a second time.

DINNER GUESTS

In St. George's when we had company—special company—we ate in the dining room. It seemed like a large room to me with its big table and chairs in dark wood. There was lots of light from two west-facing windows and from a window facing south. All looked out sea. Mom would bring out the best cutlery, white linen tablecloth and napkins, and her wedding china. She really did things up right for after the main course I "crumbed" the table with the little brush and dustpan especially for this. I had to practice before the guests came so it wouldn't look like my first time!

I realize now that my father was a gregarious man. He loved company and we frequently had unexpected guests. As Newfoundlanders, one's home was always open both for a meal or for an out-of-town friend or a relative needing a place to stay. People would arrive unannounced and would be made welcome. In some homes the table would be set with an extra place for an unknown guest!

I remember being sent to the White House, the local hotel, with a note inviting the "hikers" to dinner. It must have been 1935 or '36 and the hikers were two young men from Canada who were walking across Newfoundland on the railway track. There was no Trans-Canada Highway then! There had been progress reports in the paper for weeks it seemed, and now they were in St. George's! They were nice young men dressed in what looked like shirt, tie and jacket and wearing matching "breeks" (pants that ended just below the knee and worn with long socks). They were certainly dashing and would have looked at home on a golf course. I guess they asked the right questions because Dad held forth for quite a while as he answered their questions on the Great War, which was something he never used to talk about. I was all ears and learned a bit about what it was like although I'm sure he tailored it for young listeners.

Another special guest that I remember was an officer in the British navy. He looked fantastic in his all white uniform and peaked hat with lots of gold braid. He was the ship's surgeon from a warship that was in the harbour as part of the British navy's summer manoeuvres on our side of the Atlantic. This was a throwback to the days of Fishing Rights when there was a French presence in our area and when St. George's and area were then part of the "French Shore." Britain had to look after her interests here.

When the ships came in they were a magnificent sight—enormous compared to the usual array of craft in the harbour. They would be in for about a week and always had a VISITING DAY! What fun! The ship sent their launches for us; there were tours of the ship and visits to the canteen where we could buy goodies! I especially remember we brought back chocolate in slabs that one could dissolve in hot milk for hot chocolate (very popular while it lasted). We melted a slab of red jelly in hot water to make a Jell-O-type dessert (popular too)! Both were things I had never seen before and were not available in our two grocery stores.

These visits stopped when World War II broke out and were never resumed. We later read that both the HMS *York* and the *Dundee* were lost. We felt a kinship with those visiting sailors and wondered what had become of the crew when the ships were sunk. It brought the war closer.

DAD'S SWEETHEARTS

Beside the south window in the dining room, Dad built his bookcase. It wasn't big for he didn't have many books, but I thought it was a real addition to the room! I watched as he sawed out its space between two studs, which let out a huge pile of sawdust! It was then we learned about an old method of insulating: you fill up the space between the walls with sawdust! No doubt it had settled but must have been of some help.

I especially remember one of the books because it had a pretty cover. It was a very small book covered in lilac suede leather, a collection of essays by John Ruskin. It is inscribed "To Newfoundland from Scotland" in what looks like a female hand. In his overseas photograph album, there are pictures of Dad with a youngish woman. I somehow thought that he had had a sweetheart in Scotland. Perhaps Mom told me. I still have that little book in my collection of personal items.

There was another sweetheart on the prairies of whom I had never heard until I was about to be married. As was the custom, there was a notice in a Toronto paper announcing my upcoming marriage to Len and identifying me as the daughter of Samuel H. Butt of St. George's, Newfoundland. This notice was read by a woman who left her name and telephone number with my future mother-in-law. When I called her back, she told me she had known Dad on the prairies, but when he went back to Newfoundland she had never heard from him again. I suppose he knew it would be unworkable and felt an abrupt break was the kindest—who knows?

At any rate she must have been very fond of him as she said she told her children that at one time they might have had a Newfoundlander for a father. I felt that she would have liked us to meet. Now I would give anything for a meeting with her, but at the time I was immature and my feelings were confused as Len seemed to disapprove. I guess he felt that by telling that to her children she was being disloyal to her husband though we knew nothing of her circumstances.

I also felt that a letter from my father would have been a kinder way to end it. However, it was another time and who am I to judge? Speaking to this lady from Dad's past would have been a wonderful opportunity to learn about that period in my father's life, which is mostly a blank. I do have a couple of pictures of him in uniform posed in the door of a big pleasure boat. He is supposed to have worked for a wealthy Winnipeg family running their yacht on Lake Winnipeg.

SAMUEL H. BUTT, ENTREPRENEUR

Dad was an entrepreneur, probably by necessity in those lean times after World War I and into the twenties. Before I was born and I think before he was married, he had a gasoline business supplying fuel to the many boats in the harbour. He never spoke of it in our family conversations but according to Mother, one night there was a disastrous fire and he lost everything. Somehow a fire started in the storage yard and before long there was an enormous fireworks display as the big steel barrels of gasoline, heated to the point of exploding, shot high into the air. And, of course, as was usual at that place and time, there was no insurance. He continued the business in a modified way, which later included supplying aircraft.

I think that Dad's experience in western Canada served him well when he grew wheat the summer of '34. He knew how to stack the sheaves so they stood upright in a bundle while they dried and then to thresh them. He did this in the old barn and sawmill on our property across the road next to Uncle Hilliard's. It was no longer being used, so he spread out an old sail to cover the floor—this was his threshing floor. He'd lay down several sheaves of wheat and beat them with a flail to loosen the kernels. I thought a flail was an odd arrangement: two thick sticks were hinged together with a leather thong, which allowed the lower one to hit the sheaves with its full length thereby loosening the kernels from their husks. It was hard work to hold on to one stick and fling the lower one from over his head to hit the floor with a loud "thwack!" And it seemed to go on so long! I don't know if anyone knew what he was doing or why, but he certainly had a goal. Knowing my father and his ingenuity, he probably wanted to prove to himself that wheat could indeed be grown in Newfoundland! And the second part was that he could build a mill to grind it!

No doubt the economy in the midst of the Great Depression was an incentive. He had been an independent businessman for most of his grown-up life and saw this as an opportunity. He had always worked independently wherever he saw an opportunity or when circumstances dictated it, and he probably called on his experience on the prairies after the war to start this latest enterprise. He secured a bank loan, mortgaged the house to his sister, Mary, and her husband, Capt. William Bennett, and went to work.

All winter long, he worked in seclusion on the second floor of the canning factory developing his mill for grinding wheat kernels into cereal and flour. He didn't let anyone up there except family, who were sworn to secrecy. I think he wanted this venture to be viable before unveiling it to the public. Besides, there was an element of envy in the small community when someone did well. There were those who would see it as someone knowing more than they did and trying to appear superior. I guess it was a reaction of people whose horizons were limited. Whatever the reason, he wasn't about to expose this enterprise until he was ready. In the meantime, the family were his guinea pigs.

One day our rolled oats porridge disappeared, and we were given this gummy mass in its place! It was a coarse-ground wheat cereal that looked exactly like today's whole wheat Red River Cereal. We didn't like it but because we had no choice it gradually grew on us. In time we grew to love it. Besides the ground cereal, Dad sometimes soaked the whole kernels overnight and in the morning cooked them until they were tender and had more or less the consistency of porridge on which we put sugar and milk. It had a nutty flavour and a texture like small berries. In fact, that's how he presented them—as wheat berries. He knew how much we liked any kind of berries!

At the same time, by carrying the milling process one step further, he produced flour that looked and behaved like today's whole wheat flour.

By now his cereal was ready to be introduced to the world! In the summer of 1935, he went on a business trip across Newfoundland and succeeded in placing his "Cavell Whole Wheat Cereal" in prominent places like the Glynmill Inn in Corner Brook and Government House in St. John's (the governor's residence) as well as in many grocery stores. Friends also tried it. People were asked to try it and if they liked it to endorse it by sending him a letter including their recipes. Many did and my copy of his original flyer with a picture of me at six years old steadying a sheaf of wheat with each arm also bears several recipes and testimonials to the healthful benefits of the cereal, not least of which was its laxative qualities! He was ahead of his time in that he stressed the value of the vitamins to be found in whole wheat. They are all listed on the flyer, even some that we no longer hear about today.

As the demand grew, the family was pressed into service, filling the cellophane bags (probably about two pounds). Phyllis and I would fill these little bags and hand them over to Mom to do the weighing before sealing them and packing them for shipment. We thought this was fun; besides, it was something different and none of the kids we knew did these interesting things!

This enterprise was just getting off the ground when it collapsed with Dad's death a year and a half later. In 1937, as the Depression continued, the number of people on relief or "the dole" was increasing. A government food programme gave them credit at the local grocery stores. The government, aware of the nutritional value of whole wheat, made Dad's the sole flour provided to families whose main food in some cases was bread and tea. Dad's business of whole wheat cereal and whole wheat flour died with him and we had missed the boat!

Canning was my father's main business until he started the cereal business. Some years he canned salmon on a small scale and one year, blueberries. I don't think the berries were a big success because he didn't repeat it. At that time there was no such thing as freezing for preserving food, so canning was the technology of the times. Dad's main business was canning lobster. Lobster was considered a bottom-feeding scavenger shellfish, as was crab. North Americans didn't think it was fit to eat until around the turn of the twentieth century. How things have changed!

I'm not sure exactly when Dad started the canning business but by the time I was a small child it was in full swing. Fresh lobster was common in our house once the season started, and we ate canned lobster the rest of the year. I loved it and really missed it after we moved to Clarke's Beach on the east coast where nobody was catching them.

When I was a child, the opening of the lobster season meant the pace quickened for all of us. Dad did all the collecting himself, sometimes leaving before daylight to visit all the fishermen out along the shore and even going out around "the Cape." This was Cape St. George, which was at the end of the Port au Port Peninsula and jutted far out into the Gulf of St. Lawrence.

This was a worrisome time for Mom, especially when a wind came up. His boat was about 20–25 feet long with a "make and break" engine and was probably about six feet wide. With a full load of lobsters, it wouldn't have had much freeboard. One or two big waves coming over the gunwale would be enough to swamp it. Not only did Dad not swim (which wouldn't have helped anyhow being so far from land), but like everyone else he carried no life jackets. Newfoundland fishermen depended on their dexterity in handling the boat when there was a sea running. Their reason for not learning to swim was that it would just prolong the agony if they fell overboard! Dad had such great balance that he would entertain us by running the length of the boat along the gunwale while it was bobbing on the water!

Mom would know when he was more or less expected home, depending on how far he had to go, the amount he had to collect and the weather. We would all begin watching for his boat away out in the bay on the other side of the Sandy Point Peninsula. At that distance, his boat would be a barely discernible dot on the water. When Phyllis or I spotted a dot and Mom was sure it was him, I was sent down to the man who lived close to the factory to tell him that it was time to get the boiling tank ready. Like most people, we had no phone and the message would be sent to the women who worked there doing the packing.

By the time Dad got in with his load, the man in charge of the boiling would have filled the tank with sea water, lit the fire under it and had it boiling and ready to receive the first barrow-load of lobsters. The men carried the lobsters from the boat in an open barrow. This was an arrangement consisting of a barrel sawed in half crosswise, with handles that spanned front to back between which two men stood. They mounted two steps beside the tank and tipped their load into the boiling water.

In the meantime, Mom headed the assembly line of several women. They lined the cans with paper ready to receive the lobster meat. A man cracked the shells, some of the women extracted the meat and the others packed. Mom's job was to pick out the fine meat from the body. She was in charge of that job because it was tedious work and she was dextrous and worked fast.

The cans then went to the machine, which, after the lids were placed on the lobster meat, sealed them. The retort, a big machine that sterilized the can under pressure, came next and Dad was in charge of this because it was dangerous work. Phyllis and I were to stay out of the way and, along with our friends, eat as many lobster bodies as we could hold. We sucked the meat out of the legs and ate the tomalley (the soft green liver)—it was a feast! I have wonderful memories of lobster season!

Dad's Uncle, Sam Butt, was also in the lobster business, and was responsible for my father having the initial "H." My father had no second name and after Uncle Sam, who had none either and was his competitor, began receiving his mail one year, my dad felt it was time to do something about his name's shortcomings. He gave himself a new initial! From then on he was Samuel H. Butt.

PLANES, BLIMPS AND BOATS

Airplanes were a rarity when I was a child; if people heard one they always went outside to look. One day Dad had us all go out to look at this strange airship in the sky.

The *Hindenburg*'s journey had been in the paper, so Dad was waiting for it and made sure we all saw this phenomenon on its way to New York. Newfoundland was the shortest route from Europe to North America and as luck would have it, it travelled over St. George's! We heard later that this enormous balloon-like airship had blown up as it was landing. It was a shock!

One day to my great surprise and excitement, a plane landed in the harbour to get fuel not far from the government wharf and Dad's factory. I happened to be down there, and Dad and I hopped into the boat and went out to see what the pilot wanted. As we approached, Dad put out his hand to hold the wing to steady the boat. Immediately, the pilot shouted "Don't touch the goddamn wing!" For us swearing was a no-no; I had never heard my father say a swearword in my life and this was a shock to me. Also, the pilot had been disrespectful of Dad—another shock.

To say I had never heard Dad swear is not correct; there is one exception. One morning in lobster season he had to make a trip up to Flat Bay, an hour or so in the boat. Phyllis and I went with him. His business concluded, and we started for home. He had been up half the night and decided that as I had steered the boat many times, I could take over on the straight run home and he would get a little rest. This didn't seem that risky for we were a long way from shore and any shoals. So, he gave me a landmark to steer by and he lay down in the bottom of the boat. Soon he was asleep.

Before long I began having trouble keeping on course and, not wanting to waken him, tried to compensate. An onshore wind must have come up and even though I kept steering to the landmark, the boat continued to creep closer to the shore—and the rocks! I became confused as to which way the tiller should go. We got closer and closer to shore. I was sure I could figure it out before we got too close for it seemed to me that the shore was still quite a ways off. Suddenly there was a grating sound under the boat and our church-going, straight-laced dad sprang up with a "Jesus Christ!" and grabbed the tiller! We had drifted onto some rocks that by now were quite visible under the water. We were all scared. Somehow he got us out into safe water and we continued. He asked me what had happened but didn't scold me. The swearing was never mentioned! All he said was, "We won't mention this to Mom," and we didn't!

When motors replaced oars and sails, Dad was the first man in the harbour to have one. Motors must have been a great boon to the fishermen because not having to row meant they could go much farther and save their energy for working the fishing lines. These motors were noisy affairs, installed more or less in the middle of the boat. They had a flywheel that had to be cranked to get it to catch. They called it a "make and break" engine and it had a smoke pipe that sent the exhaust out the side of the boat.

As a young man, Dad was one of the first to have an engine in his boat and the strange loud "bung-bung" on the water gave notice that Sam Butt was out in his boat. With some people, anything different—and especially anything that they envied—brought out the worst in them. He soon had a nickname—Sammy Bung—that some people called him behind his back. He knew about this and everyone knew how much it bugged him.

One morning when I was dawdling getting dressed, Dad told me to hurry up. I had heard about his nickname at school and I was annoyed with him, so I muttered "Sammy Bung" under my breath. He heard me and I had to admit to what I had said. He went for the strap and my gentle father lost it. He got in several whacks while I screamed and jumped around on my bed trying to evade the strap. Mom rushed in from their bedroom in her nightgown, stood between us and said, "Sam, that's enough." He left, and Mom said I could stay home from school that day. Now that was sweet revenge of a sort, for being at school every day was a given and we had to have a very good reason to stay home. Perhaps I had welts that she didn't want seen in public!

Many people built their own boats, and Dad built his. Besides the regular boat used every day, he had built a much bigger one called the *Mayflower*. Now this was a special boat, painted grey with pink trim with a little cabin in the bow and her name painted on the side at the front. She must have been around 30–35 feet long and was kept on the landward side of the bank road just before one reached the factory.

This was the boat we usually took up Main River on Dad's birthday picnic, which was a big event in our lives with two or three guests invited along. Two that I remember were Miss Gillis, the postmistress, and Rev. Bursey, the minister who boarded with us. A week or so before the big event, the *Mayflower* was rolled down to the water on a succession of slender logs placed under the keel. At first she leaked but as the timbers swelled in the water, the bailing became less frequent and she became watertight. She had "plimmed." When the big day arrived, all the food would be loaded aboard, buckets for berries if we were lucky and a big kettle for boiling up. No Newfoundland picnic would be a picnic without tea—many cups of it.

THE DOMINION OF NEWFOUNDLAND

My father stuck up for his own principles and those of public interest. In 1934, just sixteen years after the conclusion of World War I, Newfoundland was deliberating on a new form of government. Newfoundland was not part of Canada until 1949 and at this time was still a separate country, the Dominion of Newfoundland, having its own government independent in most ways from Britain. It proudly called itself "Britain's oldest colony" having settlements of British fishermen and their families dating from the 1500s.

Newfoundland had lost a disproportionate number of its young men in the war and combined with its war debt and the Great Depression was on the verge of insolvency. An element of the governing class proposed the Commission of Government whereby Britain would take over the debt and rule directly from there under a British governor with eight commissioners—four British and four Newfoundlanders. Hearings were held across Newfoundland and the day they reached St. George's, Dad was ready.

A few years ago, an older man who was a boy at the time told me about it. My father arrived at the meeting in the courthouse straight from work in his work clothes and rubber boots, all the better to represent the working man. Mom was there too. He got to his feet and spoke his views on the country losing its independence; he said Newfoundland was being sold down the river by mismanaged government that was betraying the ordinary hardworking Newfoundland people and diminishing Newfoundland boys' sacrifice in the war. Dad never backed down from siding with people who were not being heard or who were not being fairly treated.

My sister, Shirley, comes by her social conscience naturally! She's been an influential English teacher, a leader of a trucking union, a tireless representative of the Labrador "Voice of Women," an organization committed to improving the lot of abused women, as well as taking a leadership role in her church.

Newfoundlanders are very nationalistic and love their country with a passion. Their national anthem bears witness to how deep this goes, and after over eighty years of living away, I still remember every word:

When sunrays crown thy pineclad hills
And summer lifts her hand,
When silvern voices tune thy rills,
We love thee smiling land.
We love thee, we love thee,
We love thee smiling land.

When blinding storm gusts fret thy shores,
And wild waves lash thy strand,
Though spindrift swirl and tempest roar,
We love thee windswept land.
We love thee. . . . .

When spreads her cloak of shimmering white
At winter's stern command,
Through frozen days and starlit nights
We love thee frozen land.
We love thee. . . . .

As loved our fathers, so we love,
Where once they stood we stand,
Their prayer we raise to heaven above
God guard thee Newfoundland.
God guard thee, God guard thee,
God guard thee, Newfoundland.

LIFE CHANGES QUICKLY

On Sundays when we didn't have to get up early, Phyllis and I would run across the kitchen to Mom and Dad's bedroom and climb into bed with them. It was cozy and felt so good to be with them where we were all squashed in together. Our parents were relaxed and there were stories and laughter.

One morning in spring as Dad got up to get dressed he looked out the window and exclaimed, "Come quick and see! There are baby chicks out here!" Baby chicks were one of our loves, so we sprang out of bed to see! When we looked out the window to see nothing but the bare boards of the bridge (deck), he doubled over with laughter and said, "April Fools!" We thought it wasn't funny, as telling the truth was very important in our house and here he was lying. He explained it was all right to fool people up until twelve o'clock! Afterwards we always tried to fool him and each other but rarely did it work as everyone was ready.

Jumping into bed with Mom and Dad was also a chance to see his war wounds, which made me feel prickly down the backs of my legs, they were so awful. He really didn't want to show us but with a bit of coaxing, he always did. There was one deep gouge under his right shoulder blade that we could lay half our hand in. The other one was in the small of his back on the left side and was much deeper and longer. They were deep purple-red and covered with a thin skin that was almost transparent. Just looking at them told the story of his suffering. He kept one of the pieces of shrapnel removed from his back on his shaving washstand! It was mounted on a rounded dark wood base.

He volunteered on the day that news of the Beaumont Hamel slaughter reached St. George's. On July 1, 1916, on the Somme salient, the Royal Newfoundland Regiment was sent to take the village of Beaumont Hamel, a German stronghold. When the day was over the target had been taken and out of the 600 Newfoundlanders that went "over the top," less than 100 answered roll call the next morning; the rest were dead or wounded.

July 1 is Remembrance Day in Newfoundland, a day of reflection. It's Canada Day in the rest of the country, a time for celebration.

On that day, according to his sister, Mary, Dad had been out in the boat and when he reached shore and was told the news, he said, "Someone has to take their place," and went immediately up to the courthouse and volunteered.

He was wounded at Ypres in 1917 where the Allies had been dug in. He never spoke of it, but Mom told us about it later. Their position was being shelled and when the men in Dad's trench heard the scream of the shell coming over they flung themselves down, one on top of the other. When the shell exploded and the shrapnel flew, the topmost soldier in the pile was killed as was the one under him. Next was Dad whose back was ripped open and the one under him escaped. Sometime later when the ceasefire was called to let both sides gather up their wounded, someone dragged him, unconscious, into the first aid area where the wounded and dying were lying all around. The less badly wounded—the ones who had a chance of surviving—were treated first.

Dad lay unconscious under a bench all night, and in the morning when someone noticed that he was still breathing, it was his turn for some attention. His ears and wounds were packed with battlefield mud, which had stopped the bleeding and actually saved him. However, this was mud that horses and men had died in and must have been teeming with tetanus. He escaped that too. Another soldier was given the job of syringing out his ears. Diluted carbolic acid was the antiseptic of choice on the battlefield but undiluted carbolic was what Dad got in his ear by mistake. The ensuing pain brought him to but damaged that ear for life.

According to his army records, he arrived at the battlefield on July 2, 1917, and was wounded eight days later on July 10. The blast that almost killed him likely saved his life for he was invalided to hospital in England for the next four months and later convalesced for a year before being sent home and discharged. For the rest of his life, his left ear frequently suffered infection, which was referred to as "runny ear," and Mother made him a padded shield to wear over it in the wind and cold.

One bitterly cold day in January, Dad's Uncle Alfred, his mother's brother, appeared at our door at dinner (lunch) asking if Dad would take him back to Sandy Point with a calf he had just bought. Naturally, Dad was glad to help out and after the meal they headed for the boat. It was a cold, windy day and on the way home the wind was blowing straight into his weak ear. He realized when he reached into his pocket for the shield that he didn't have it with him. That night he began to have pain in that ear and in a few days was really sick. With the condition not improving the doctor was worried that the infection was spreading to the mastoid bone, which was the big danger in ear infections, so he sent Dad to the hospital in Corner Brook. They operated to create drainage and the big cavity that had been created behind his ear was packed. Doctors hoped the infection would subside. There was nothing else that could be done in those days before antibiotics.

As the days went by and the hospital bill that they couldn't afford mounted, Dad wrote Mom a letter, which I still have. In it he speaks of being well treated, of his friends the Bartletts coming to visit, of his concern that Mom will be needing more firewood and whom to call about it, of missing her and the children.

After a week or so in hospital, it became apparent that he was not getting better and the infection was spreading. His thinking and memory were affected so he signed himself out. He probably knew that he wouldn't survive and wanted to be with his family.

Mom was sitting in the rocker beside the window when she saw a man she didn't recognize staggering down the field toward the house. As she and her visitor watched him she recognized Dad—who was wearing a strange leather helmet with earflaps—and flew out of the house to his side. She got him in, warmed him up, put him to bed and sent for the doctor. By then the infection was spreading and turning into encephalitis engulfing his brain.

We were sent outside to play whenever the doctor came to change the dressing, but I hung around the window where I could see what was going on inside. I watched as the doctor pulled what seemed like feet of packing from a huge hole in his head behind his ear. I knew then that it must be serious.

To make matters worse, his speech centre had been affected and he couldn't find the words to communicate so many important things to Mom. Dad would call out from the bedroom on the same floor that he had something important to tell her, but when she got there he couldn't find the words he needed. His frustration was enormous, and he would shake his head and almost cry. She was sure that he was trying to tell her important things, so the frustration was equally great for her. Our mother knew nothing of the family finances as Dad hadn't wanted her to worry. She knew nothing of the mortgage on the house or the bank loan, which was the normal way of doing business when he had embarked on the bold venture of the cereal business.

They had promised each other that they would each tell the other one if they were going to die, and Mom kept her promise. She told us she agonized over how to do this. She screwed up her courage and went into the bedroom and said, "Sam, do you think you are going to get better?" He knew what she meant and turned his head to the wall.

Despite the loving care from all of us, within a week he was dead. It was simply unbelievable, and everyone was in shock.

The butterscotch colour of the ice on Norman Butt's field the week our dad died is still vivid in my memory almost eighty years later. I also remember not being allowed to go out to that ice to go sliding after he died. At that time and place it would have been seen as unseemly and of not showing respect for the dead. I remember thinking that Dad would be OK with it. I couldn't see how play could be disrespectful!

How the big wind-up kitchen clock dragged its hands on those two days before the funeral on the third day. The green darkening blinds were drawn to the windowsill and the whole house was in gloom. In the parlour, Dad lay in his coffin resting between two chairs. People who had come to pay their respects would be taken in to see him by either Mom or Aunt Mary who had come to help.

Before the visiting began, there were certain women in the community who attended to the "laying out" of the deceased. They would come and wash and dress the body in its best clothes after which the coffin would be taken to the "best" room. I don't remember this part happening to Dad, but I remember being taken to the parlour by Mom to see him. He was in his blue suit, the one he wore every Sunday—probably the one he'd been married in ten years earlier. It was unbelievable to see him lying there with the faintest smile on his lips, and I had to keep telling myself that it really was Dad lying there. There was such a sense of loss—I can still feel it. He wasn't just off on a business trip like last year; now he was gone for good and I would never, ever see him again! Afterwards, I cried many times but never around Mom because that would start her crying, which was scary.

A couple of days before he died, Mom told Phyllis and me that "Daddy wasn't going to get better," so we were warned, but it didn't really sink in. He died in the early morning of Feb 4, 1937. In the morning she came into our room and told us that "Daddy had gone to heaven." We knew what that meant and burst out crying—much is a blur, but I do know I turned away and stood behind the bedroom door just crying. I don't remember ever talking about it to Phyllis—it was too big for us to put into words; we just moped around.

Aunt Mary, who had come a few days before, held things together and the day of the funeral she took Phyllis and me in tow for the funeral service held in the parlour. Mom held two-year-old Shirley in her arms. When it was over, Aunt Mary had Phyllis and me "kiss Daddy goodbye." I didn't want to do it because that body wasn't the same Dad I knew. My feelings were confused. I didn't know where he was, but I was sure he wasn't in that cold body. I can still remember how cold his forehead felt to my lips. It seems cruel to put young children through that, but we certainly got closure.

When everyone left for the cemetery, we weren't allowed to go—it was a very cold winter's day and I'm sure the family felt it would only add to the sadness of the day. My mother stayed with us but suddenly the house was empty, and the loneliness was overwhelming. Through the bathroom window upstairs I watched the long line of people make their way slowly up through the field to the road where the horse and sleigh waited. I was nine and a half years old, and my world had changed forever.

THE AFTERMATH

In the next day or so, Mom and Aunt Mary went down to the factory to take stock of the situation there. I was left in charge of the two younger ones. I don't think I had ever been alone with the other children for any length of time before but there seemed to be some urgency, even secrecy, to their going. We weren't supposed to tell anyone where they had gone. I now know that Aunt Mary wanted to get her bid in first as Dad had mortgaged the house and property to them to get the cereal business off the ground and there was also an outstanding business loan at the bank for the same purpose.

Anyway, the time dragged. We spent our time looking out the window towards the factory. I remember the harbour and the wharf where they had gone was solid with ice. In our minds, ice was dangerous, people fell through it every year and were drowned. We had been taught to stay away from it and now our mother was down there in that dangerous place! As time went by my imagination had her falling through the ice and never coming back. Now we were REALLY alone and, being the eldest and in charge, I was terrified in a different way from the others. I thought of going down to the factory to find them but realised I couldn't because I was looking after Phyllis and Shirley. There was no telephone. I was getting really desperate when I saw a strange man walking down the lane beside our property. I tore out through the snow and begged him to go tell Mom to come home. Mom and Aunt Mary returned before long and a feeling of relief and protection took over.

Mom cried all the time it seemed and as we had never seen her cry before we were even more upset. We never cried in front of her as we thought that would only make things worse. Shirley cried a lot, too, and kept asking when Dad was coming home. She was two and a half and couldn't understand it.

Phyllis and I started back to school. It felt different; I felt different. I felt like I had lost part of myself and that took getting used to. It felt like it was something I had to work on to feel complete again.

It must have been a terrible time for Mom. There was no money coming in, we needed to buy firewood and the grocery bill at Arnold Morris' kept climbing. Mom was so distracted that she didn't hear us when we spoke to her, she repeated herself, she was always crying, she lost fifty pounds and in short was going to pieces. As the pressures of the financial situation built, a new worry appeared.

One day she took Phyllis and me aside and told us that because we didn't have a father to support us anymore that we might have to go to the orphanage in St. John's. She didn't want to do it, but it would be a way of our being clothed and fed. This was something else that made us feel insecure and it was pretty scary. In her sixties, Phyllis spoke of how worried she had been. Ours was a house in which we never spoke of feelings because that would spell weakness.

Aunt Bessie in St. John's had read Mom's rambling letters and was worried about her. When she received a letter from Aunt Mary saying that if she ever expected to see her sister again, she should come and get her, Uncle Jim came to size up the situation. The idea was put forward that Mom should pack things up and go back to her family on the east coast. We would live in Grandma Norman's house in Clarke's Beach and Mom would be with her own family.

Shortly after Uncle Jim left, Mother asked me to keep a secret. We were leaving St. George's in May. I felt very grown-up and didn't tell even Phyllis. Mom started to gather up things and store them in a corner of the parlour. One thing in particular that struck me was a feather bed that she rolled up and sewed into a cover. It hit me then that we were really going.

The year before, Mom and we children had gone to St. John's for a holiday to visit Aunt Bessie and Grandma. It was her first time home since coming to St. George's to be married ten years before. I loved the trip. I loved travelling on the train, seeing the countryside whizz by and eating our sandwiches for every meal. We were still travelling when we woke up in St. John's.

Before long, Mom had Aunt Mary come and they decided what Mom could take with us. Before they were married, Dad had bought the house from his brother, Uncle Stan, who had returned from Canada and was living with his bedridden mother and looking after her until she died in 1920. It was furnished mostly with my grandparents' things that they had inherited or items they had purchased after their marriage in 1867. I imagine it looked pretty much as it had in their day and as most things were in working order, Mom and Dad had added very little.

Dad had made a couch that sat along the kitchen wall next to their bedroom. It was really a locker, for the seat lifted up to reveal compartments for storage and we kept things like jam and cans of lobster there for the winter. That was ours and she didn't have to ask for that. There was also a wardrobe cum cupboard that Dad had made for Mom to put all her flowering plants in at bedtime so they wouldn't freeze; keeping that was a given. She was very proud of her flowers and had a "green thumb." This filled the corner of Phyllis' and my bedroom and it was also where we hung our clothes.

So, Mom was clearing with Aunt Mary which of the family pieces she could take with her. I trailed around after them and heard her ask Aunt Mary for Grandma Butt's sewing machine so she could make the girls' clothes. It was a treadle machine and a more up to date one than Grandma Norman's, which had a handle on the wheel that one turned by hand while trying to keep the cloth running through the machine with the other. She also asked for the harmonium so her girls could learn to play. This was a four-octave organ that was portable and went to church on Sunday mornings in our grandparents' horse and buggy. After the service it came back and sat in the dining room all week where most of the children learned to play it. Grandpa Nat had brought it home from New York in his schooner.

I guess I picked up on Mom's apprehension, for I remember holding my breath that Aunt Mary might say "no" and we wouldn't be able to take these essential pieces with us. But it all worked out and these things were crated to go.

LEAVING ST. GEORGE'S

Mom had a focus now and a way out of her dilemma, so the mood of the house improved as plans were made. Also, Uncle Jim made inquiries on our behalf to the Great War Veterans' Association regarding a widow and orphans' pension. There wasn't too much available in the thirties, but they came up with thirty dollars a month; fifteen for the mother and five dollars for each of the children.

So, things moved ahead for our departure. I was torn as I had enjoyed Clarke's Beach on our visit last year, but St. George's was home. In St. George's, I had the sea that I loved and which I would have to leave. One evening just before dark, I walked down to Uncle Hilliard's wharf, walked out on it and stood there to say goodbye to the sea. I had a deep knowing that I would never again live in such proximity. I shed a few tears and went back to the house.

A few days later, one night in early May, we left St. George's. We closed the door and walked up through the field to the road. Like all our neighbours we didn't lock the door. I don't remember if I looked back but that big old house looking out to sea is still home to me.

We walked the short way to the station agent's house which was near the station and were bedded down on the couch. We were roused at three o'clock in the morning and made our way to the station in the dark with Mom carrying Shirley in a blanket. Within a few minutes the train rolled in, we climbed aboard, and the train began to move. As it gradually picked up speed, the last of St. George's and home were left behind. We had begun a new chapter. Shirley had just turned three, Phyllis was seven, and I was nine.

Clarke's Beach, our new home, was an overnight train journey away and we were about to begin a new life: the second phase in my Life's Journey.

Part 2

CLARKE'S BEACH, NEWFOUNDLAND, 1937–1942

My Second Home

PICKING UP THE PIECES

After a night and day on the train we arrived in St. John's and were met by Aunt Bessie. We were a motley crew. I have a snapshot of our family and Aunt Bessie standing in front of her house. Mom, who had been a fairly heavy person the year before, was little more than a skeleton wearing her one "good" dress, which just hung on her. Phyllis and I stood like zombies with drooping heads and downcast eyes. Shirley, who had just had her third birthday, also looked sober. Life was still full of unknowns but at least we were still together. The threat of the orphanage was now behind us.

The two-hour car ride around Conception Bay to Clarke's Beach was exciting, for we weren't used to being in a car. Boat had been our main form of transportation when Dad was alive.

Grandma Norman awaited us. I'm sure a houseful of young active girls wasn't her idea of a way to spend her seventies, but she made us feel welcome. Grandma Norman had a heart problem and was not too active, though she returned to her home every summer and stayed until late fall when she went to her daughter's in St. John's for the winter—and central heating! I'm sure she loved the peace, quiet and space of the country.

Emma Jane Dawe, my maternal grandmother, had come as a bride to this house from the small fishing village of Port de Grave, three or four miles down the shore of Conception Bay. With my Grandfather Robert

Norman she had eight children—two dying in infancy, which wasn't unusual in those days. It was the custom that the youngest son and his wife would make their home with his parents and look after the parents in their old age, inheriting the property when they died. This my grandparents did.

My Grandpa Norman, like many men of that time when the only employment was fishing, "went to the Labrador" in the summer. Once the schooner, powered by sail, arrived at the fishing grounds, the summer was spent on the water. Small dories containing two men put out from the mother ship before daylight and jigged codfish all day by hand. In the long northern evenings, they fished till dark, then forked their load onto the ship from a rocking dory, no small feat in rough water. Work didn't stop there as the fish had to be split, cleaned and layered with salt until the catch could be dried later. Then they could eat their only meal since breakfast and catch a few hours' sleep before daybreak when they were once again on the water. Lunch would be a cake of hard bread in a man's pocket, which didn't provide many calories for the rest of the day. It was back-breaking work but with no opportunities for anything else, it was a living.

My mother was the seventh child born into a family of eight children. First came four boys then four girls. Around the time when my mother was due, her sister Marcella (Marcie) developed "summer complaint" (dysentery), a not uncommon problem for young children and one which was dangerous due to dehydration. People didn't know what caused it or how to cure it. My Aunt Bessie was four and her baby sister was two. Playing with the toddler outside in the fresh air and feeding her fresh blueberries that grew in the garden was Aunt Bessie's way of helping out. Fresh fruit was scarce but was known to be good for people, so the sick child was given as much as she would eat. With all that roughage she became sicker, and the day my grandmother gave birth to my mother, her two-year-old died.

Many years later, a cousin who had lived near them told me that my grandmother stayed in bed the better part of a year after that and my grandfather kept the house going. These days it would likely be seen as postpartum depression. No wonder! My grandmother bore another daughter two years later who died in infancy.

So, our lives settled into a new pace when we reached Clarke's Beach. Ours was a houseful of females, even the cat, "Floss", was part of the sisterhood! They were generally happy years for us as our mother didn't dwell on what we didn't have. True, we didn't have a father anymore, and though we missed him a lot, I'm sure she missed him even more.

CLARKE'S BEACH

Clarke's Beach on the east coast of Newfoundland had a very different culture from the west coast.

The first thing I noticed was that the people sounded different—they had a different way of speaking both in their expressions and their accent. This area was the first English settlement in the New World with many villages dating from the 1500s, including Port de Grave where my grandmother was from. Even in the first half of the twentieth century, in isolated villages in coves and bays where the only contact was by water, one could tell where a person was from by their accent. Although many of these differences disappeared when the Trans-Canada Highway and television came in the fifties, I can still spot the occasional accent, especially the ones from the north coast!

Newfoundlanders are a very open-hearted people, helpful to others and welcoming in their homes. When Phyllis and I as seven- and nine-year-olds would run up the road to visit our neighbours, the Normans, the first thing they told us was never to knock! We learned that to knock was to consider the occupants as strangers and unwelcoming, and that was frowned upon. We would burst in through the door and seat ourselves on either side of the wood-stove and remain wordless as did they if they were at our table. We all felt comfortable and we were always welcome.

Sometimes Mr. Norman, Old Will (as his son was young Will), after a bit of coaxing, would play a tune on his tin whistle or accordion for us. We loved it. We later learned that Old Will was a first cousin of my mother. Eighty years later, living in my retirement home in Toronto, a visiting minister came to conduct service. His name was William Norman! On seeing this announcement, I knew I should check this man out! On the appointed day, I went to the auditorium to wait for him. After he had settled himself and after introducing myself, I told him that his name was a familiar one in my family and asked where his father was from. "Newfoundland" was his answer! My second question was "What part?" When he said Clarke's Beach and gave me the same address as the house next door, I was floored!—and we were cousins!! We later got together, and I was able to tell him many things about his family that were new to him.

MAKING ENDS MEET

Once we were set up in Clarke's Beach, Mom managed by buying as little as possible at the grocery store, growing all our own vegetables, making all our clothes. After a couple of years, once we had electricity, we didn't turn on the light in the kitchen until almost dark. Mom made it a routine for all of us to sit in the kitchen (which was also our living room) as it grew dark in order to enjoy the twilight. We grew to love the twilight and we didn't know it was an economising device!

Another strategy was to let the fire go out when we went to bed. Lots of families "banked" their stoves to continue the heat longer into the night, but not us. Mom said she was afraid of a house fire with all of us upstairs; I guess that could have been part of it. But boy was it cold at night! Phyllis and I slept together in a northwest bedroom and I can still see the curtains blowing in the draft that came through the cracks around the window. There were no storm windows in our community. We had homemade quilts but not enough of them. Some had some wool patches in them, but not many. Phyllis and I slept with our backs touching to share the body heat and I guess it helped some. Even though we each took a big flat beach rock to bed that had spent the day in the oven, I was on the outside and still cold.

When we got up in the morning, Mom had the fire going and a big pot of porridge and homemade toast with our own blueberry or partridge berry jam ready for breakfast. We had enough to eat and we counted our blessings. I don't remember complaining of the cold bed. We knew of a family up our road where the children didn't have shoes or socks.

We arrived in May, which meant the potatoes had to be planted for the winter supply as well as turnips and cabbage. After the leftover potatoes had been brought up from the root cellar, Mom and I (at almost ten) cut them up so that each piece would have two to three "eyes" that would sprout once planted. The planting took a couple of days. I felt very grown-up doing this grown-up work beside my mother. Mom, Phyllis and I each carried a bucket of these and laid them carefully in the drills that the neighbour had ploughed with his horse. He then returned to cover them up and came a second time about a month later once we had laid a capelin on either side of the small plants. Phyllis and I felt very important doing this adult work!

We also dried some of these tiny capelin for our use come winter. There was a big pile of rocks down in the meadow that we called "the wall" where we spread some spruce boughs so the air could get under the capelin and dry them. Capelin are a tiny fish about the size of a smelt and are plentiful in North Atlantic waters. At a certain time in the early summer, the coves of eastern Newfoundland are on the receiving end of the capelin runs. The females come inshore to shallow water to release their eggs, and the males fertilize them. The frenzy in the water saw uncounted numbers being flung onto the beach for children to fill their buckets when I was a child. There were so many capelin next to the shore that they could be scooped up in buckets by men and women with or without rubber boots. It was an exciting time as they gathered it for either food or to fertilize their gardens. These days when the word is out that the capelin are in in some village or other, many people go there to see the action as it is a unique phenomenon. Not many people use them in their gardens anymore as we did when my mother would contract with a man with a horse to bring us a wagon load.

In the fall, the routine was reversed as we were all involved in digging the potatoes and dumping them down into the root cellar. Children helped according to their strength and felt an important part of the family. A lilac tree that Grandma had planted years before was at the corner of the kitchen garden where the fence met the deck outside the back door. It was in bloom shortly after our arrival and I had never smelled anything so heavenly! In St. George's nobody had a flower like that, and it contributed to my emerging feeling that Clarke's Beach wasn't such a bad place after all! When the apple tree and a purple plum tree came into bloom and later when we had the fruit to eat, we felt blessed. She had grown both trees herself from an apple seed and a plum pit!

Mom planted carrots, turnips and cabbage for the staple dinner of corned beef and cabbage (which we all loved) in the fenced kitchen garden. The beets would be pickled later in the winter as a treat. We ate lettuce with a sprinkling of sugar, but the tomatoes had be picked green as they were slow to ripen before the season closed in. Newfoundland has a boreal climate so even though it gets more sunlight in its northern location, the season closes in sooner. We wrapped the tomatoes in newspaper and stored them in a dark drawer. Phyllis and I could hardly wait and checked them constantly, which probably delayed them, but what a treat!

One day a car stopped at our house—a rare occurrence! When we reached the front door, there to our surprise was our old friend Bob Milley who had boarded with us several years before in St. George's. It was wonderful to connect with him again. He was on his honeymoon. At Christmas time, a large four pound box of chocolates arrived from Bob and we children were overjoyed. It was a rare treat, and Mom rationed us to one a day, which saw them last a long time! When the beautiful blue box from Robertson Bros. was empty we used it for storing our snapshots for years.

Years later, when Len and I were about to be married, he took me to his great- grandfather's home to meet family. It was the home of one of the Robertson brothers, Alexander, now deceased, whose daughter, Jessie, Len's grandmother, had brought up Len after his parents divorced. Small world!

SETTLING IN

Next on Mom's list for attention was the barn that had been built by my great grandfather when they first moved up from Port de Grave nearly 100 years before. It was past repairing, so Mom had the neighbours (Norman relatives) build a new one where the goats and chickens went at night and where the hay went up to the loft toward the end of the summer. Ours was not a farm but simply a way of life that most people followed to survive in a small rural community.

To feed the goats during the summer, we milked them in the morning and then turned them loose to feed off the grass in the nearby hills. On the way, they might decide that the grass inside someone's fence looked appetizing and with their horns locked inside a paling, they could snap it off in a minute. There was a way of foiling this activity. A device made of three boards or sticks nailed together called a "yoke" was placed around their necks and thus the goats were denied the juicy vegetables in someone's garden before they took to the high rocky hills behind our property.

For Phyllis and me their journey to the hills was a big "groan," for every evening we would have to bring them back for milking and the night. We would set off for the ten- to fifteen-minute climb into the hills to find them there with a lot of their friends. They would answer to their names but took off when we got closer so that we had to chase them to cut them off and direct them home. We developed pretty strong legs!

Once we were home, the milking had to be done and I, wanting to demonstrate how grown-up I was, usually took this on. We usually got a quart from the two of them, which was just enough to put in our tea and on our porridge in the morning. We had to stretch this amount as Shirley, who was only three, needed milk and my mother was very concerned about this. When the goats dried up for a month or more preceding the arrival of their kids, she bought a whiskey bottle full of milk from a family with a cow. Phyllis and I really missed our cow in St. George's where we had loads of milk, cream and butter.

In the late winter we would check first thing in the morning to see if any kids had been born that night. I still love kids with their sweet little faces. They are so fun-loving, leaping on and off things, tossing their heads from side to side.

A more sober side was that one of them would become our meat in the winter after the frost was deep enough to keep it frozen—usually a billy goat. A neighbour would do the deed behind the house and hang the carcass from a rafter in the cellar-workshop where we would have to dodge it going down the ladder to where the vegetables were stored! I hated it, but that was life!

When planning to kill an animal for food, many people followed the old practice of killing it on the rising of the moon so the roast wouldn't shrink. The belief was that if it were killed on the waning of the moon, it would. The same practice applied to the spring planting when people would wait until the moon was rising before sowing the seeds.

This was our only fresh meat unless Mom bought a rabbit from some man who, fresh from his snares in the nearby woods, came to the door with a brace (pair) hanging over his shoulder. Rabbit stew was a real treat cooked in Grandma's iron bake pot and we all had our favourite parts. Phyllis and I would argue as to whose turn it was to get the head as we both loved the tasty brain.

The general store carried salt meat, which was kept in brine, and we loved it boiled with potatoes, cabbage, turnip and figgy duff (a pudding boiled in a bag with the dinner instead of baking it). Many families ate this on their dinner plate along with the main course, but we used to have it as a dessert with a sweet allspice sauce. Much later in Toronto, Newfoundland boiled dinner was always a favourite with my own four boys, one way of my connecting them with their Newfoundland heritage.

Chicken was a rare treat for dinner as to kill one meant fewer eggs and was done only after some consideration. Only the older ones whose laying was diminishing met the axe. I'll never forget the day little Shirley came tearing into our house saying the hens had escaped from the chicken yard and were eating the rat poison that Mom had put out for a rat she had seen. It would be a disaster to lose our precious hens, and besides we wouldn't even be able to eat them—or so one would think if they didn't know our mother! She set us to catching the hens in the fenced-in yard. There were three of us and at least fourteen or fifteen of them. The bedlam was unimaginable as we lunged for the squawking and terrified hens. When we caught one we would run with it to Mom who stood by the chopping block, axe in hand. She would open its beak and sniff for a sulphur smell and if it was there the chickens lost their heads on the spot! If there was no smell of the poison, back they went into the chicken yard. Once all were sorted out, Mom drew the unlucky ones and examined the entrails. If the poison laced bread had not gotten past their craw and farther on to the intestines where the absorption takes place they were safe to eat. All but a couple passed the test—we had acted quickly enough! For the next couple of days, we ate wonderful chicken stew and the remainder was bottled for later. My children see me as a practical person—I wonder where that comes from?

FISH TALES

In the spring we fished in North River, which ran behind the properties on the other side of the road. We would have preferred a light, flexible bamboo pole that was sold in our general store but that would have raised the grocery bill. Mom directed us to ask Mr. Seward who had a wooded property across the road if we could cut a pole there. After a lot of searching, Phyllis and I settled on two young, tall, thin spruce trees and chopped them down. They were still green and heavy and thick, but we skinned off the bark, attached the fishing line and were in business.

To go trouting in the long spring night after supper, we had to have done our homework; it was amazing how quickly that could be done! After doing the dishes and digging the worms, we tore off down the road, across the neighbour's property and down the hill to the river. It didn't take long to get the hook in the water. The red and white bobber floated and supported the sinker with its baited hook a few feet down. We hoped it would be irresistible to the population there!

At the end of a good evening we could be carrying home a "skiver" (a short piece of a spruce branch) full of tomorrow's supper—flatfish (flounder), speckled trout, salmon peel (year old salmon) and eel. All fresh and delicious. They all had to be gutted and skinned, which wasn't my favourite job, but not wanting to tarnish my emerging image as a reliable hard worker, I wasn't about to complain!

Speaking of my image as a reliable teenager, the winter I was thirteen I took to getting up first, jumping into my icy clothes, lighting a fire in the kitchen stove and carrying a lighted lantern to the barn through the snow to milk the two goats. My mom had been looking after my ailing, bedridden grandmother all winter and it was my way of helping out.

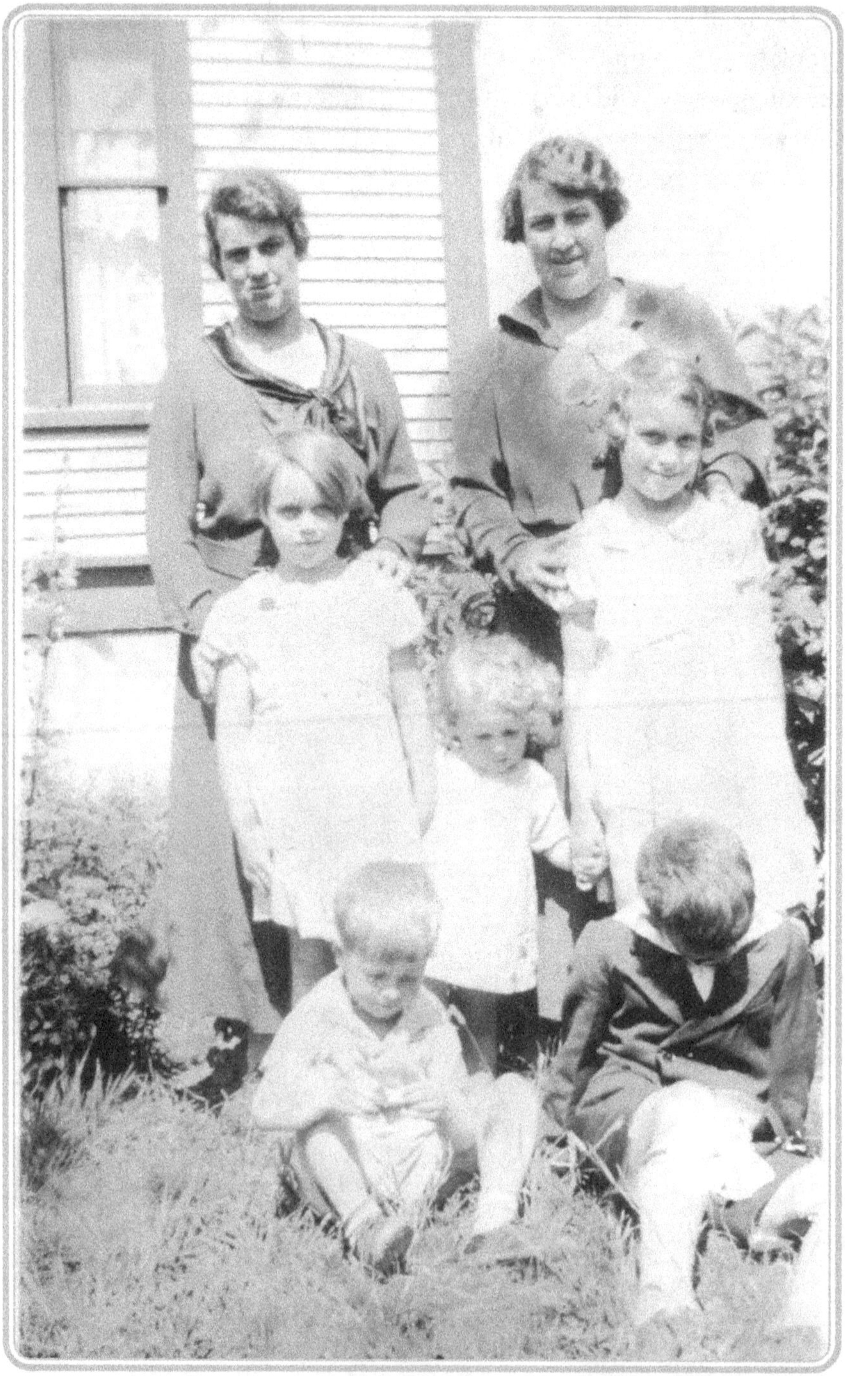

Arrival in St John's: 1937, family and Aunt Bessie

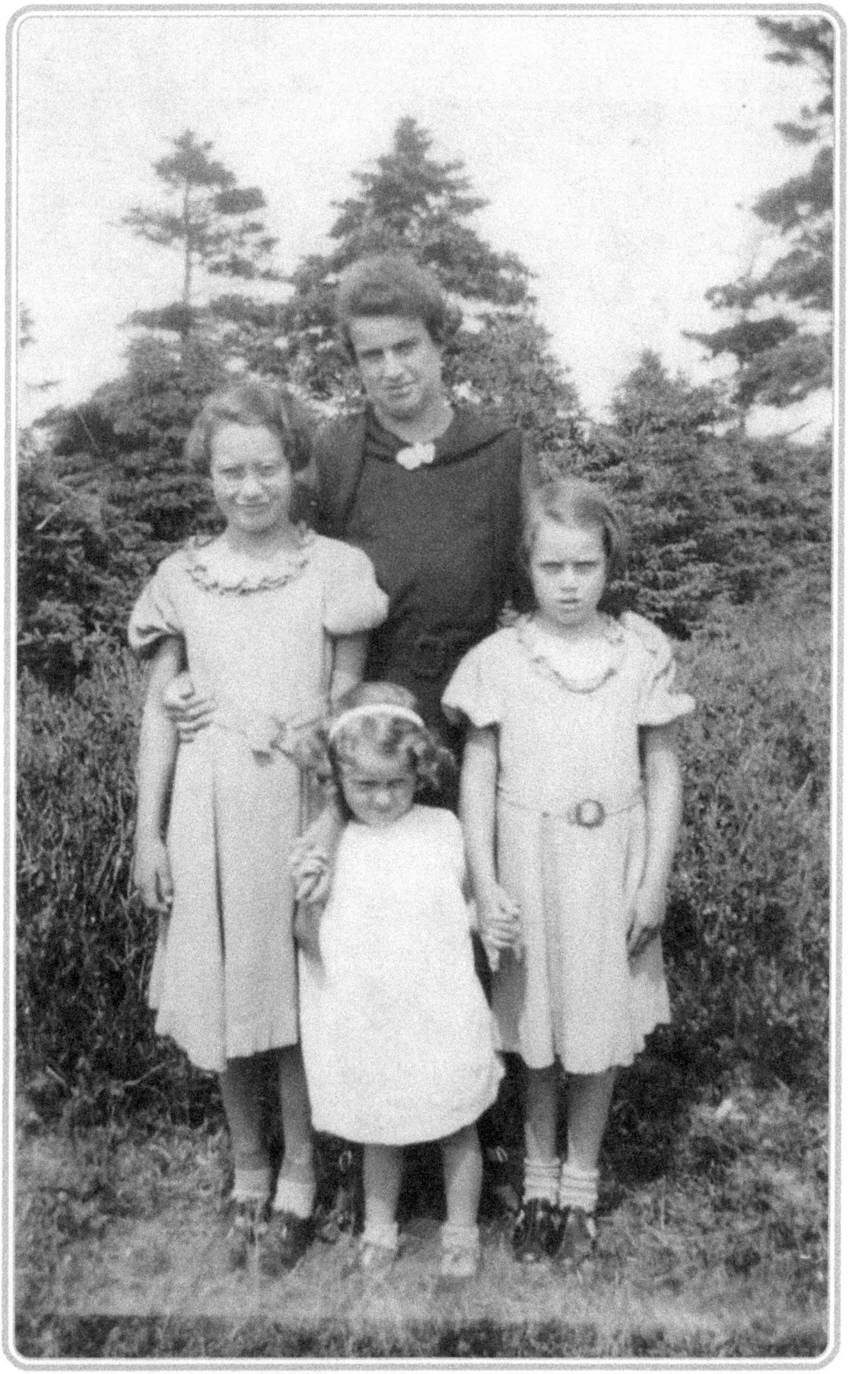

Mom and 3 girls: 1938

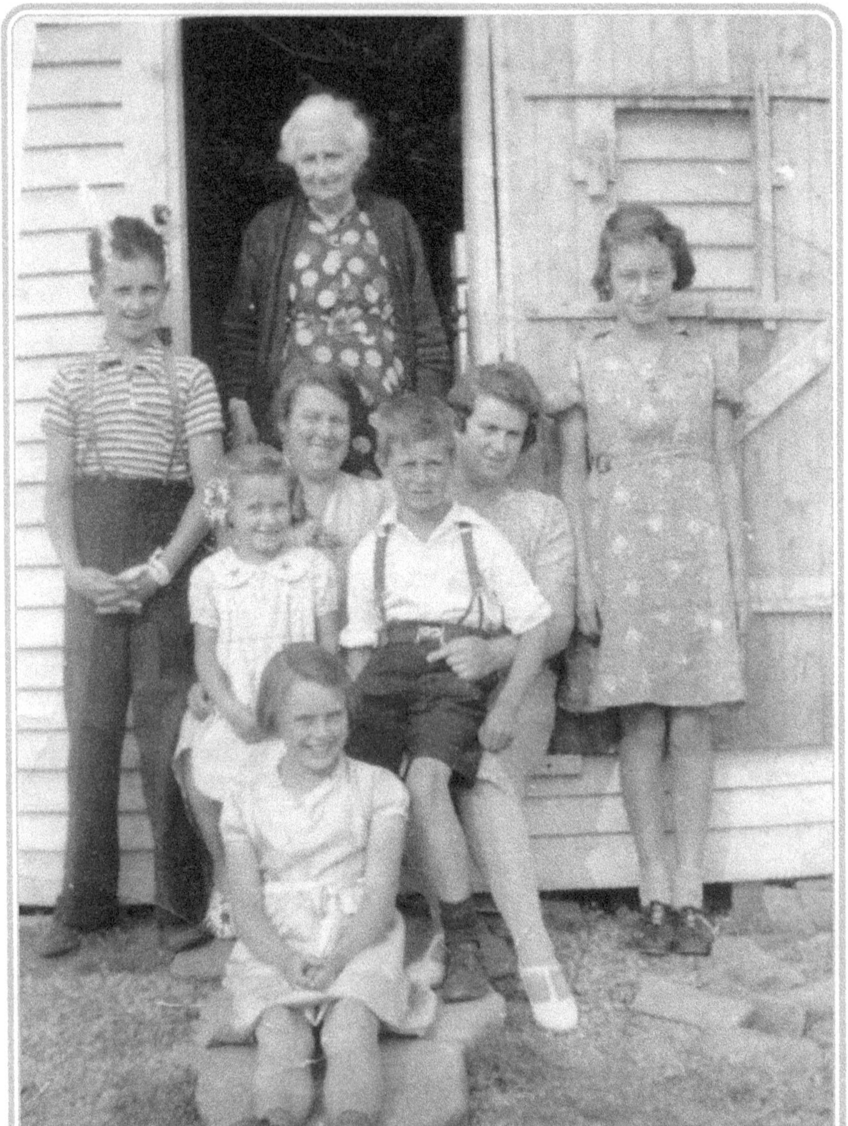

Hodgewater Line: family gathering with Grandma Norman

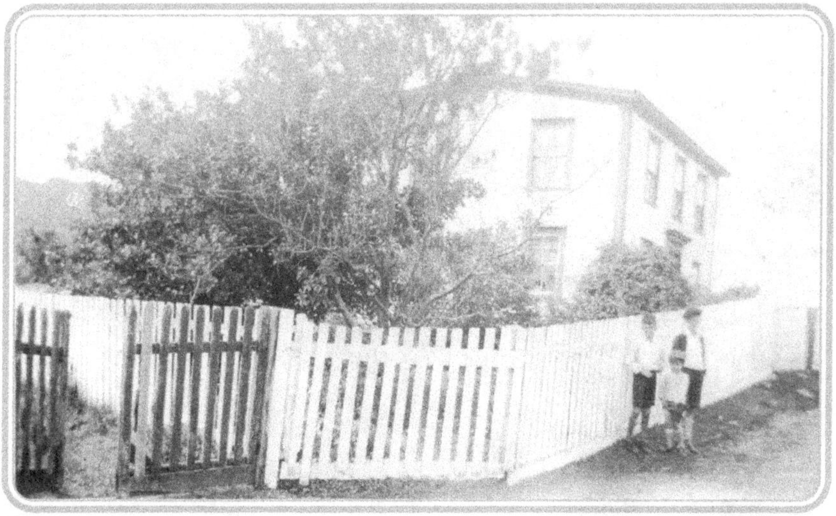

Grandma Norman House in Clarke's Beach

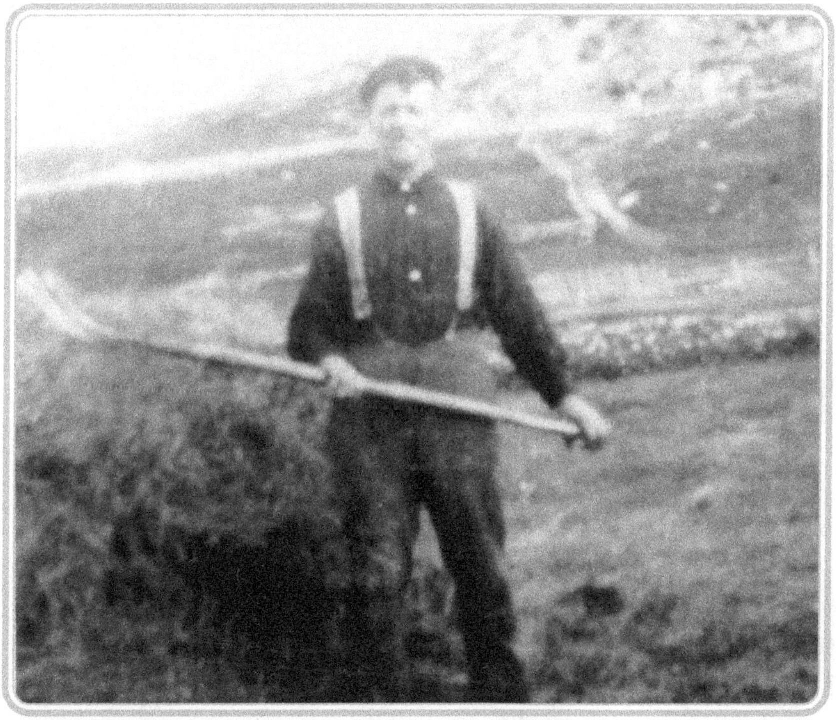

Grandpa Norman haying with 'Bald Rock' behind.

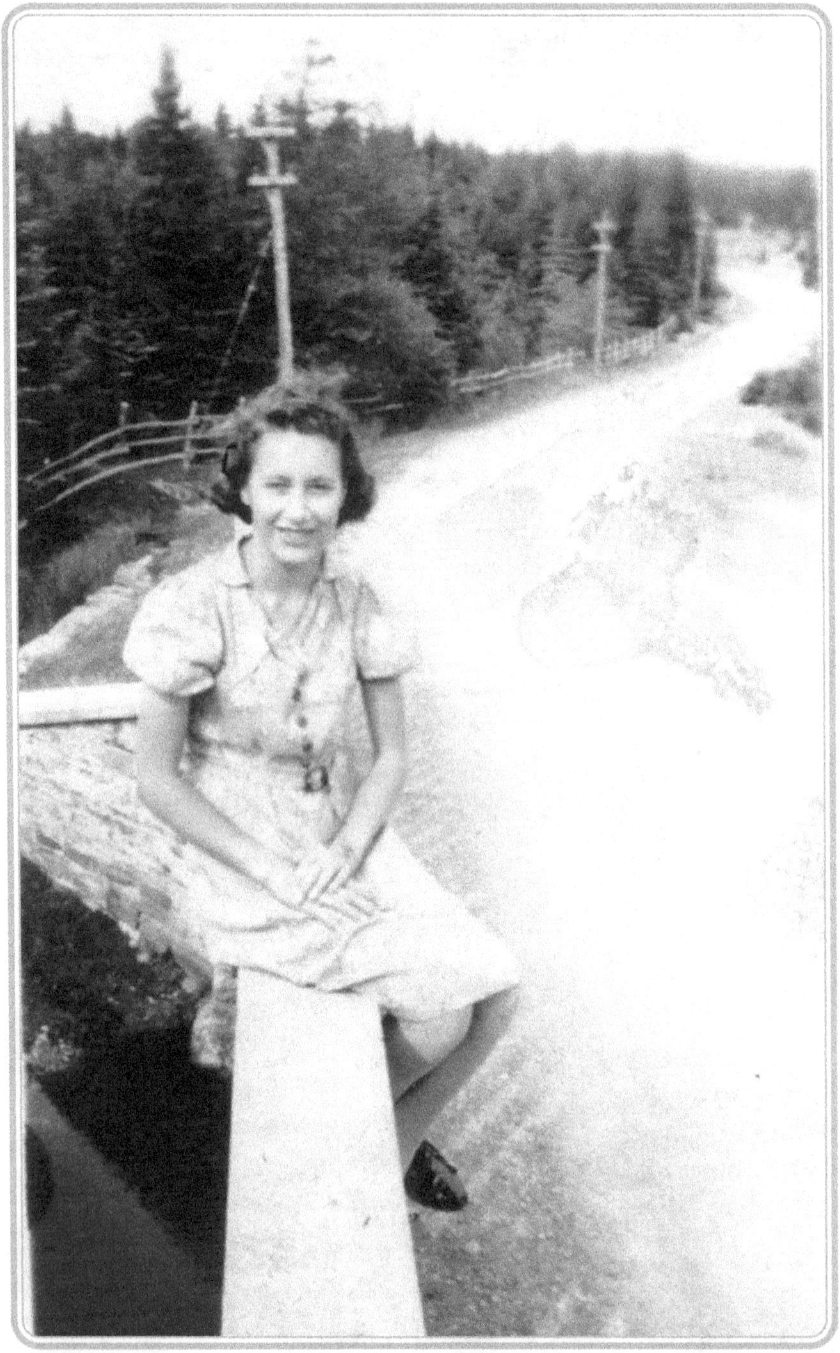

Cavell, Mt Pearl, 1941

A2 THE GLOBE AND MAIL • FRIDAY, OCTOBER 14, 2016

MOMENT IN TIME

SS Caribou sunk by a torpedo

CAME TO CANADA ON "CARIBOU" AUG 14-15 - 2 MONTHS ~~LATER~~ EARLIER 1942

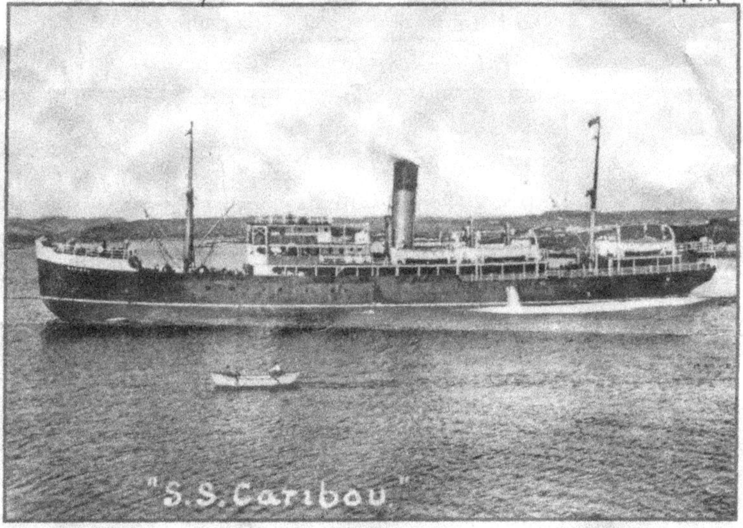

THE ROOMS PROVINCIAL ARCHIVES DIVISION

Oct. 14, 1942 | After the United States entered the Second World War, German naval attacks in the North Atlantic accelerated, with U-boats sinking several navy and merchant vessels in the Gulf of St. Lawrence. On a dark, moonless Wednesday morning in the fall of 1942, just before 4 a.m., U-69 fired a torpedo at the SS Caribou, a passenger ferry heading from North Sydney, N.S., to Port aux Basques, Nfld. The ship sank in about five minutes, killing 137 people, including 10 children. The 101 survivors who had made it onto lifeboats or clung to wreckage were eventually picked up by the HMCS Grandmere – the naval minesweeper that had been escorting the Caribou – after it had diverted to pursue the attacking sub. In a war that was largely fought elsewhere, this was the deadliest attack in home waters. – *Richard Blackwell*

Passenger ferry 'Caribou' torpedoed, 1942

SCHOOL IN CLARKE'S BEACH

School was a mile up the Glam Road and across on the Beach Road. In winter there was always snow on the ground, sometimes up to our knees. On those mornings we would be elated if we could hear the bells of a horse and sleigh in the distance for we could jump on the back runners and get a ride.

At lunch-time we would walk home, eat our cooked dinner, wash the dishes and walk the mile back to school all in an hour and a half. I'm sure our mother thought it good training in organizing our time, but we would be late if we didn't run. We generally didn't dawdle!

There was a radio programme at noon that we wouldn't miss called *The Barrelman,* which "made Newfoundland better known to Newfoundlanders." Onboard a schooner, a barrel would be fastened high up on the main mast and a sailor would be assigned to climb up and keep a lookout to give the captain information. He was the "Barrelman" and was depended on for the latest information regarding what was happening on the sea. This radio programme gathered stories from many people about events and exploits of all kinds and was always fascinating. The radio personality presenting this programme was Joseph Smallwood who, many years later as premier of Newfoundland, brought Newfoundland into Confederation as Canada's tenth province.

I would have loved to have a bicycle. I learned to ride on my cousin Bob's bike in St. John's the year before and it seemed to me that a bike would be a real advantage in Clarke's Beach to get me to school sooner. A friend at school let me ride around on hers. I loved it. It wasn't a "go" as Mom would have had to buy two, and that was impossible in our situation.

In Clarke's Beach ours was a two-room school. One room was for grades up to five and the other was for grades six to eleven, which was our matriculation year. Our materials came from England, so there was a lot of English content in the English and grammar courses. There were upwards of twenty students with all grades taught in the same room. It certainly taught me how to concentrate as well as how to learn from the lessons of others. By the time I studied *Macbeth* in Toronto a few years later, it was my third time hearing it. I knew it inside out!

The room was heated by a big pot-bellied stove in the centre of the room. If your seat was too close, you cooked, and if too far away you froze.

One year there was hot cocoa for everyone at recess time (government, I guess) and I was the one chosen to make it. The stove heated a big pot of water and then in went a can of Carnation milk, maybe two, followed by a paste of sugar and cocoa. We all looked forward to this treat and likely for most of us it was all the milk we got for the day. Afterward, we rinsed our cups in a fresh pot of water and put them away in our desks for the next day. There were no concerns about spreading disease although TB was in many homes; but we were lucky!

We had a huge map of North America on the far wall that pulled down like a roller blind. I loved geography. Here I was on the farthest eastern edge of North America and there on the very far west coast was Vancouver. I guess I had the travel bug even then as I told myself that one day I would go there. I did just that years and many experiences later, where I met my husband.

OUR AILING MOTHER

In the fall of 1941, Mom told us she had to go to the local cottage hospital for some tests. It was probably just before Christmas when the results came back from Canada. Mom was then sent to hospital in St. John's and we went to stay with relatives. Phyllis and Shirley went to St. John's with Aunt Bessie and I went to Bell Island with Uncle Bob and his family. Before long the word came that Mom would be going to St. Anthony where there was "radium" for treating her "tumour." Nobody used the word "cancer" in those days. It was only whispered.

St. Anthony is at the very tip of Newfoundland's Great Northern Peninsula. These days it's known for being close to the first Viking site in North America at L'Anse aux Meadows. In 1942 it was, and still is, the home base of the Grenfell Mission, which gave medical help to the people on the isolated coasts of Labrador and northern Newfoundland. Because of Dr. Grenfell's connections, St. Anthony had the only cancer treatment facility in Newfoundland.

Mom was sent on the long trip on the supply steamer on its last voyage before freeze up. It was Christmas and we wouldn't see her again until the first boat south in the spring when the ice had gone out. She arrived back in St. John's on Mother's Day, the second Sunday in May. Aunt Bessie and Shirley went to the train to meet her. The train drew to a stop and Shirley, who could hardly wait to see her long gone mother, raced the length of the platform checking all the windows as she went. No mother. She then retraced her steps slowly and saw a hand waving in a train window. The face behind it was gaunt and wasn't like the mother who had left five months before! Mom slowly alighted from the train, sank into Aunt Bessie's car and as soon as they reached the house went to bed.

On Bell Island, where I had spent the winter, I was given the news that she was home, and arrangements were made to take the boat to St. John's the next day. I tore upstairs to see my mother as soon as we arrived. It was the biggest shock of my life. She was a shell of the robust woman I had last seen at Christmas, and my face must have shown it. I couldn't believe a person could have changed so much in those few months. She was very thin and now had white hair. She was very warm and sweet, not like the usual no-nonsense person I had known. I'm sure she knew her time was limited. I didn't.

I was wearing a summer dress with a hem I had let down myself as I had seen my mom do many times. She asked who had done it and when I told her I had, she looked proud. She also asked if I had any money. When I said no she went into her purse and gave me a dime saying that girls my age should have money in their pockets. It felt like things had changed between us; I was no longer the child I had been.

By midweek we were on our way "around the bay" to Clarke's Beach and home. Mom must have been exhausted. We all pitched in to open the house that had waited for us all winter—it hadn't even been locked. Our neighbours, the Normans, had looked after the goats and hens, and we had a new kid too. The bad news was that our friend Floss the cat had died of wounds she had sustained in a fight. We were all sad.

It was almost the middle of May and time for the potatoes to be planted. The neighbours came to our aid and one morning three or four men turned up, got the potatoes up from the cellar and spent the morning cutting them for seed.

Mom, with help from us, cooked a big salt meat dinner with vegetables from the cellar complete with a boiled "pudding duff" for dessert, topped with partridge berry sauce. What a treat! We carried it out to the little hill beyond the well and had a picnic. It felt like a fun time and Mom's health seemed to take a back seat though she must have been exhausted.

Because Mom was so weak, she needed help to keep things going at home and the decision was made to keep Phyllis home from school to help her. One of the jobs Phyllis was assigned was to freshen up the picket fence around the house so it would look well cared for at the funeral! No doubt it was ready for its annual coat of lime whitewash and even in these circumstances it was important for Mom that her family not look hard-up. At barely thirteen, Phyllis took on the jobs of an adult: cooking, cleaning and doing the laundry on a scrubbing board in a washtub of water brought from the well!

Meanwhile, I continued at school and tried to study knowing there was a lot riding on the country-wide exams in about six weeks; it was essential that I pass.

Mom had shared with us how we would help each other to get educated. The summer school fee to train to be a teacher cost $100. As the eldest, once I began teaching and earning an income, I would save the $100 for Phyllis' training and she in turn would finance Shirley. Mom had it all figured out. After Mom died, we found $60 of the $100 in her trunk. She must have done a lot of economising to get that amount together. It probably accounted for the occasional time we had porridge at suppertime though she had made it sound like a treat!

On the home front, Mom was failing and could no longer get out of bed. She could only drink sips of orange juice we squeezed for her from a dozen oranges that her friend Mrs. French had brought. Mrs. French had severe arthritis and could scarcely walk so it must have taken enormous effort on her part. I wonder now whether it was heartening or not for Mom to have these friends coming to say goodbye. Knowing how far a walk it was from the main part of town would also convey to her the message of how near her end was.

Mom sent me twice to find the public health nurse so she could get a shot of pain medication for her newly developed bowel obstruction. I had to walk miles around town leaving messages and trying to find her. The nurse could have been anywhere and there was no phone. Both times she came to Mom's relief.

One day Aunt Bessie came to stay with us. We learned that Mom was dying and wouldn't be with us much longer. It finally registered. The word cancer had never been spoken and, to me, "tumour" was something serious but people lived with it. Guess I didn't want to acknowledge what was staring me in the face. It was something one dealt with internally, and Phyllis and I never spoke of it though we both were worried. Once I dropped in on a new family I had come to know and shed my tears there.

I had those exams coming up on Monday. I walked the mile and a half to the Roman Catholic school at North River where the exams were held every day for a week. I came home for dinner at noon and went back for the second exam that day. I wrote my last exam on Friday afternoon. On Friday evening, Mom's brothers, Tom and Rob, both of whom had arrived on the train that day, gathered with Aunt Bessie, Phyllis, Shirley and me in Mom's room where she gave us away to our relatives. I was to go to Uncle Bob on Bell Island, Phyllis to Uncle Tom in Botwood halfway across Newfoundland, and Shirley to St. John's with Aunt Bessie. It was a pretty sombre scene but at least she had avoided the orphanage for us once again. It must have taken a lot of courage, for she loved us so. She lost consciousness that night and died the next morning. She was thirty-nine.

I think she had waited until my exams were over because it was an important part of her plan.

I passed.

STARTING OVER AGAIN

After the funeral, Aunt Bessie took my two sisters, Phyllis (13) and Shirley (8) to her home in St. John's. Phyllis soon went on to Uncle Tom's in Botwood, while Shirley stayed with Aunt Bessie. Shirley must have felt so alone having just lost her mother and within weeks both her sisters when we moved away. She had been treated most leniently by Mom who more than once described her as a "poor little fatherless child." On her arrival at Aunt Bessie's house, she found that approach to childrearing was over.

Her boy cousin, Norman, only slightly older, was the favourite in that household and Shirley suffered. Not only that, Shirley was a very bright student and all her life stood first or second in the first rate school she attended. She outshone her cousin and that must have made things difficult too. She graduated with a scholarship, but she wasn't allowed to accept because it was seen as charity by Aunt Bessie; it must have hurt. However, she graduated from teachers' college and later earned a BA while teaching. In Aunt Bessie's old age, Shirley was a caring daughter to her much more so than her own sons.

I was fifteen and stayed behind in Clarke's Beach with my mother's cousin, Jack Fillier, and his family who had offered to take me when Uncle Rob couldn't due to his large family. I wasn't that sorry as the noise from all the children was intense and I had to sleep three to a bed with my girl cousins. The Filliers were to be my new home, but it soon became apparent that I wasn't welcome. They already had two children, a teenage son and a daughter who was Shirley's age. Jack's wife, Ada, worked hard in the house and although I was used to helping with all the work at home, she wouldn't let me help. She never spoke to me. I didn't feel welcome, so I spent a lot of time helping another cousin who was visiting for the summer. I hardly knew her but wanted to feel useful somewhere. I found myself walking around town a lot and dropping in on people I knew. I was looking for stability I suppose.

I felt lost.

Word must have gotten back to Aunt Bessie in St. John's about the Fillier arrangement not working, and she came to visit. She told me that Mrs. Butler, whom I hardly knew, had offered to take me. She ran a small store out of her house and felt she could use my help after school. Mrs. Butler also had a teenage son and Aunt Bessie probably thought that would not be the best situation for me with hormones in the picture, so she declined the invitation.

Aunt Bessie must have been desperate to find a home for me. For whatever reason Mom had emphasized that she didn't want us to go to our father's family so Aunt Bessie now faced a real problem. She probably felt that despite Mom's earlier wishes, Dad's family should step up to the plate and help settle one of the Butt orphans. She must have called Aunt Ruth Morris, my father's sister, who lived just outside of St. John's in Mt. Pearl, which was as yet undeveloped. Mom and we three girls had exchanged visits a couple of times since Aunt Ruth and some of her family had moved back from Toronto the year before, so we knew the family somewhat.

Before moving to Toronto, she and her husband, Uncle Roll Morris, had lived for many years just outside of St. John's in a small house they had built just inside a large wooded property they owned that stretched from one highway, up the hill to the next. On their return from Toronto, Uncle Roll and his son, Harold, set up a sawmill, cleared the property, sold the lumber and sold lots on streets in Mt. Pearl, which they named after some of the Morris children: Ruth, Norma, Alice!

The lumber went to build Fort Pepperell, the new American army base on the then outskirts of St. John's, on the far side of small Quidi Vidi Lake. It was one of the three American bases in Newfoundland that were part of Churchill's and Roosevelt's Atlantic Charter "lend-lease" arrangements that they had worked out on a naval ship in Placentia Bay. It was 1941 and Britain was staggering under Hitler's growing bombardments both on land and at sea. The Dominion of Newfoundland, not yet a part of Canada, saw an enormous amount of American activity as we were the closest part of North America to Europe. Churchill gave the United States ninety-nine year leases (free) in three locations in Newfoundland that were jointly governed by Britain and Newfoundland. Bases were built in Argentia on the south coast, a naval base; an air force base at Stephenville on the west coast; and an army base in St. John's on the east coast. They have since reverted back to Canada but at the time, I remember American uniforms were everywhere. The intermarriage with Newfoundland girls accounts for the hundreds of Americans who have Newfoundland grandmothers!

Beyond the effect on the US's and Britain's war effort, the charter also spoke of self-determination for countries whose independence had been taken away (no doubt due to the European war), but it has since been credited with inspiring countries such as India and many African countries toward their own freedom. The US did not declare war until the Japanese attack on Pearl Harbour in Hawaii on Dec 7, 1941.

BIG LIFE CHANGES

Nothing changed for me for another two or three weeks until the next time Aunt Bessie came. She had a letter for me! I had never received one before, and I was excited as I tore it open. It was an invitation from Uncle Stan to live with his family in Toronto. It felt heaven sent. Not only would I have a home, but it would be in TORONTO!! Toronto had always been the Promised Land in our family. Aunt Bessie had gone there in her early twenties and worked at Eaton's. My mother had done the same as had their brothers, Will and Harry. Harry still lived there. I eagerly looked forward to it!

So, Aunt Bessie took me to St. John's to wait for a friend who was soon travelling to Toronto and would keep me company en route. But another surprise was just around the corner: within a few days I came down with chicken pox and I was really, really sick. I had pox all over my body, even in my hair. When I had almost recovered, though still a bit shaky, I said goodbye to my eight-year-old sister, Shirley, and boarded the train. I didn't see her again for three years.

JOURNEY WEST

I felt the momentum of the beginning of a huge life change.

As the train entered the countryside, my green felt hat flew out the open window. People laughed, but I was upset. It had been new the year before and matched my best dress that Mom had made for me. I had been taught to look after my things. Later, I saw the loss of my precious hat as an omen of my move to a new life. Besides going to a new family, I was leaving the country I loved. Even at a young age, Newfoundlanders were proud of their country, the land and its heritage.

I stopped off at St. George's, where I'd had my first experience of leaving home when I was nine years old, for a couple of days. I was now fifteen and had never gotten over the homesickness I felt when we left after Dad died. It was like a dream to walk from the station to the big old house by the sea that I knew so well.

Dad's sister, Aunt Mary, lived in the house now and nothing physical had changed as far as I could see. But everything I had known had changed. It was home no longer, no parents, no sisters. I felt empty.

I went to visit my cousin and old playmate, Audrey. What a change, for she was now married with a new baby! Even so, it brought back poignant memories of my childhood and our close friendship. It was so good to see her again as I had dreamed many times of being with her while living hundreds of miles away.

Although I had recently lost my mother, I wasn't wearing any signs of mourning, so Aunt Mary decided to remedy this breach of etiquette (as she saw it). She pinned a broad band of black cloth on my coat sleeve. I wasn't happy with this decision, but I didn't have any choice. My mother had not imposed this on us when my father died, and as soon as I got on the train out of St. George's I tore it off.

We arrived in Port aux Basques late in the evening to catch the midnight boat to North Sydney and Canada. There was a long line of passengers showing their passports or visas, as Newfoundland would not be part of Canada for seven more years. When it was my turn all I had was the letter from Uncle Stan indicating that I would be making my home with them. It wasn't good enough for the Canadian Customs officer because I had no visa! It suddenly occurred to me that a second cousin of Dad's had once visited us years before and had stayed overnight. I would have been only around seven or eight years old, but I remembered his name was Lou Davis and that he worked for Customs in Port aux Basques. I asked if he was available and found that he was on duty in the next booth! He looked at the letter and at me and, having heard of my family situation, vouched for me. I was on my way to Canada!

A VOYAGE TO REMEMBER

All was in darkness as we boarded the *Beothic* for North Sydney, Nova Scotia. No lights were showing as it was wartime and Newfoundland had already had several sinkings from U-boats. There was a routine on entering the cabin. On opening the door, one was immediately faced with a thick, black, floor length curtain which could only be opened after closing the door. The portholes were also shuttered. All this was reversed on leaving the cabin.

We went out on deck as the boat left. It was very dark as I watched the unlit houses of Port aux Basques that were silhouetted against the sky disappear. I felt I was leaving everything I had ever known—what was left of my family, my friends, both my hometowns, my country. My feeling of loss was mixed with the excitement of entering this new period of my life. I was fifteen.

The danger of lurking submarines was also at the top of my concerns, as just a few months before I had heard the explosions of torpedoes from the U-boats when they had sunk two iron ore carriers at Bell Island where I was living. Also, I had just left St. John's, which, as the most north-easterly land on the continent, was a busy port. As it was the closest land to Europe, ships of all kinds—naval and cargo bound for wartime Britain—assembled their protected convoys there. Naval ships hunting ever-present submarines put into St. John's, which was heavily fortified against attacks. A submarine net was underwater, mines were at the narrow harbour entrance and there were manned fortifications on land. These had been shelled, and Newfoundland was very much a war zone. The ship I was standing on would be sunk by a U-boat a few weeks later with a great loss of life. The vulnerability that I was feeling during that overnight crossing was well founded!

As I stood there remembering all this, I suddenly felt a warm trickle running down my abdomen under my underwear and quickly made for the washroom. The abscess that had been festering on my breast ever since the chicken pox had finally burst. What a mess. I cleaned up the best I could with the toilet paper (which bore a close resemblance to waxed paper). I remember feeling somewhat besieged as I dealt with this latest assault. It was more of a complete letting go than I had expected!

Aunt Bessie's friend and I slept fitfully that night and arrived at North Sydney early the next morning. The train was waiting for us. Soon we were underway for Toronto. I was now in Canada and what struck me most was the height of the trees! Being from Newfoundland where the land was boreal and the trees relatively small, I was really impressed. The landscape flew by and I think I must have been a bit overwhelmed by everything, especially what awaited me in Toronto, for I remember very little of trip. The trip was uneventful—a day and a night and it was soon over. A new life in Canada was about to begin!

Part 3

CANADA, 1942–2020

My Third Home

MY ARRIVAL

Toronto was in the middle of a heat-wave when I arrived on August 15, 1942. It was HOT. I had never experienced such heat. I was used to 70F being a hot day at home. In Toronto it was in the 90s!

My widow mother had died a few weeks before, and I was responding to an invitation from my father's brother, Uncle Stan Butt, to live with his family in Toronto. I didn't know this family—there had never been any communication between their family and ours, though we knew who they were.

I arrived in Toronto early on a Saturday morning. The taxi pulled up to 216 Spadina Road just as Aunt Alice, Uncle Stan's wife, was getting into her friend's car to go to work. I said goodbye to Aunt Bessie's friend who had kept me under her wing and entered my new home for the next phase of my journey: two and a half years in a brand new setting.

Waiting inside were Uncle Stan, Iris and Marjorie, my cousins. They were older than I, Marjorie by six months and Iris by two years. They were very warm, kissing me and running for Kleenex when my eyes overflowed. I had never seen Kleenex before; I was only familiar with cotton handkerchiefs. And I had come from a culture where people didn't kiss and hug. In fact, I can't remember ever being kissed by my parents. Only babies and small children were hugged, and I was uncomfortable with this new custom.

That Saturday was memorable. I was shown my room on the third floor, which the three of us shared. There were three single beds, which meant I had a bed of my own! I couldn't believe it as I had never slept by myself in my life. At home, I had always shared a bed with Phyllis. Sometimes when staying at Aunt Bessie's or Uncle Bob's we slept three to a bed, which wasn't unusual. It also kept people warmer in the winter in unheated houses!

I unpacked my few things. There wasn't much in my suitcase. Trying to remember now, there would have only been two or three dresses, a couple of underpants, a pair of stockings, an extra undershirt, but no bra. The women in my family didn't wear bras. If a woman wore a corset, as my mother sometimes did, it had a built-in bra. Bras were a relatively new fashion as far as my family and I were concerned, and this must have seemed odd to my cousins who had extra bras and a closet full of clothes. I realize now that at home we had had only the bare essentials, though I had never felt deprived.

Mom had made all our clothes, including new coats—one for summer and one for winter—which we wore when we went to school and church and which did us a second year when the hem was let down. The coats were worn in all kinds of weather. We didn't have raincoats or umbrellas, and I always hoped that my coat would dry out a bit before I had to put it back on to walk to or from school. If it felt cold we could count on the walk to warm us up. By the time we had walked the half hour home for lunch (our dinner) we were OK.

My pride and joy was the smart "grown-up" summer coat that Aunt Bessie had made for me that spring after Mom died. There was also the new sweater that Mom had knitted for me while she was in hospital. It was a raspberry coloured cardigan with embroidered flowers down the front—the latest thing—and the buttons were Inuit style: narrow triangular strips of leather rolled into tight buttons, common in the far north. I loved it and wore it for many years.

SHOPPING

My wardrobe was about to expand; we all piled into the car and drove downtown to Eaton's to buy a new dress for me. I was a bit overwhelmed by their generosity and by the racks of new dresses. I had only ever had clothes my mother made—sometimes from new fabric but frequently from one of her own. I was mesmerized, but Marjorie pulled three or four dresses from the racks and guided me to the dressing room to try them on! I had never heard of such a thing but soon narrowed the choice down to a simple navy blue with a lace yolk. I had never had such a pretty dress in my life, and I couldn't get over the fact that one could take home more than one and bring back whatever didn't work!

We then went to a Chinese restaurant for lunch. I had never eaten in a restaurant and I guess it really was a special occasion for them as this was the only time we ever went to a restaurant as a family! The food was strange, and I didn't eat very much. With all that was going on that morning I didn't have much of an appetite. Uncle Stan seemed to know the waiter as he kept calling him "Charlie" so I thought the family must come here often! In the early forties, there wasn't much respect for visible minorities and certain people called Chinese men "Charlie" after an individual in a movie. It wasn't meant to be respectful, and people like Uncle Stan thought it amusing.

SETTLING IN

For the first week in the oppressive, sticky, August heat of Toronto, I lay in the large hammock on the front verandah under the huge maple tree that covered the front yard. I could spend the day reading! I gobbled up the copious reading material as at home I had only been used to the *Star Weekly* from a friend after her family was finished with it. This was a bonanza!

When we arrived at Grandma Norman's house in Clarke's Beach five years earlier, I had found three books in the bottom of the kitchen cupboard: *Titanic*, *Swiss Family Robinson* and *Anne of Green Gables*, all of which I devoured. They were the only books there except for schoolbooks. So, in Toronto I was excited to have all this reading material and to be able to read all day! By the end of the week I had regained my strength and got more involved with my cousins, who showed me around the neighbourhood and took me to Sunnyside, an amusement park in the west end next to Lake Ontario. It was there that I was introduced to a roller coaster. I was terrified and vowed never again! Years later in Disneyworld, I endured a well-disguised roller coaster ride with my excited children!

The food at my new home was wonderful; fresh meat at every dinner, and dessert too! We had rarely had dessert at home, mostly it was bread and jam. Cake was a treat. Mom always had a fruitcake reserved to be served with tea when visitors came, but it wasn't for family meals. This was the custom in many homes, and hostesses were never caught short when unexpected visitors dropped in!

I had always been slim, even thin, and began to gain weight with all the milk and Aunt Alice's copious menu. I did have trouble with the unfamiliar flavours of celery and cantaloupe, but not for long! Occasionally we had ice cream for dessert after someone volunteered to go to the drugstore to pick it up. At that time most kitchens had an ice box for keeping food cool but not frozen. The ice was delivered once a week in twenty-five- or fifty-pound blocks. Refrigerators soon appeared in homes after the war when they were again being manufactured; factories no longer made wartime products like tanks and munitions.

We were invited to Marjorie Richardson's for dinner the next weekend. She was Aunt Mary Bennett's (Dad's sister) daughter who had married in Toronto and had a little daughter, Marie Christine, who was around four or five. It was wartime and Marjorie boarded an English couple who had a daughter the same age as Marie Christine. It was arranged that my cousin, Marjorie Butt, and I were to stay the week and take the children to nearby Kew Beach Park on the shore of Lake Ontario every afternoon. The children were bored as they couldn't play in the sand while wearing their beautiful starched dresses! No doubt we were a help to Marjorie, but I hated chasing children all afternoon and was glad when I could get back to the house and read!

The next weekend the family had a picnic on Centre Island. WE WERE ON THE WATER and I was in seventh heaven! It wasn't the type of shoreline where I could wade, but I loved jumping from rock to rock just at the waterline. I was nine years old again and felt so alive. Aunt Nellie and Aunt Lula, Aunt Alice's cousins, were with us and they welcomed me with a box of chocolates. When we got home I invited Iris and Marjorie to have a chocolate, but they refused saying they were mine only and no amount of persuading could change their minds. I was a bit bewildered as I had been brought up to share everything. The chocolates lasted a long time!

As a baby, Aunt Alice had been brought up with Aunts Lula and Nellie in Toronto when her own mother had died in Newfoundland. I now wonder how much that fact had been part of the decision to invite me to Toronto. It wasn't something that we ever discussed. They accepted me as another niece, and Aunt Nellie sewed and knitted for me as she did for Iris and Marjorie. My first gift was a wine skirt and a hand-knitted grey sweater for school—I was thrilled, for I had always wanted a skirt with a waistband like the ones in the Eaton's catalogue and not attached to a top like my mother always made. I now felt much more grown-up! Aunt Nellie and Aunt Lula always remained part of my family.

FAMILY LIFE

The next week, Aunt Alice went on holiday from the munitions plant where she worked. She was a hard worker and the idea of sitting around for a week was not in her nature. She had cleaned houses during the Depression when there was no work for Uncle Stan, and she still had a couple of long-time customers. So, when her holidays from the munitions plant came up, she decided to take a job as a chambermaid in one of the hotels in Muskoka. That was vacation country and her afternoons would be free to enjoy the gorgeous lake with its woods and islands. Many years later, after her divorce from Uncle Stan, she and her second husband, Bill Winkworth, bought a property on the mainland looking over the lake. It was a lovely old house and was where the staff from one of the big hotels had lived.

Anyhow, the family was on its own with Uncle Stan doing the cooking (having declined my offer to help). I hated feeling useless; somehow it diminished me not to have any responsibilities.

Probably the second or third morning after Aunt Alice left, when I came down to what I thought was the empty kitchen, I was grabbed as I went into the pantry. It was Uncle Stan, concealed behind the pantry door, who pinned my arms to the side and planted a big sloppy kiss with his big lips squarely on mine. When I could pull my head back a few inches I looked him straight in the eye and said, "Be like a father, Uncle Stan," and broke away. It was the second time in a month that I had endured this kind of behaviour!

At Aunt Bessie's just before my leaving Newfoundland, there were friends in for the evening, one of whom was a former student who was home from Canada. During the evening there was a singsong with everybody crowded behind the piano and me standing at the back. Suddenly the visiting student, a middle aged man, came up behind me and put his hands on my breasts!

I froze.

To get away from him would have created a commotion, which I felt would backfire on me when the group singing would have been interrupted. I also felt he would have denied it if I had been brave enough to say what had happened. No matter what I did I could have been the disrupter and liar.

So here I was in my new home in Toronto with a new problem—the person who was supposed to be my protector!! For the next two and a half years I kept my distance and he never tried anything again. I managed the problem myself and never told anyone as I felt it would cause trouble in the family and perhaps also for me.

SCHOOL

School started within three weeks. Iris and Marjorie argued about whose school I should attend. Marjorie attended Northern Technical as it was then known (now Northern Secondary) while Iris went to Oakwood Collegiate, a regular academic school. Oakwood was my choice, and I attended there for the next three years.

By September the mornings were chilly, and I was surprised by the change in the weather. Iris and I walked the block south to catch the streetcar at the corner of Dupont and Spadina. She saved my life many times before I learned that one had to check for cars before stepping off the curb! That had never been a problem on our country road back home!

I began my first day at Oakwood by going to the principal's office to register. Mr. Hanna, the principal, came to the counter to talk to me. I had the copy of my report from the Newfoundland Department of Education saying I had passed the country wide Grade 10 exams. I therefore expected to go on to Grade 11, which at home would have been matriculation from high school. I discovered that matric happened at the end of Grade 12 and that most students continued for another year for senior matric.

After our initial discussion Mr. Hanna asked me how old I was. I had just had my fifteenth birthday a few weeks before so he felt I should go into Grade 10 along with the other fifteen year olds. I had skipped a couple of early grades, which made me young for Grade 11. I was devastated at the thought of repeating a year because it was just not in the books for me, especially with my new home situation. I had always scored near or at the top of my class and had passed the country-wide exams while my mother was dying. I felt if I could do that I should not have to repeat my year, and the principal gave in. I now know he was right. The different system and without the grounding in a couple of subjects meant that taking Grade 13 at seventeen years old was a bit of a struggle.

Physics and chemistry were hard, but French was terrible. I was OK with the grammar and vocabulary, but my pronunciation was English style. I had never spoken French. When my time came to read aloud I baulked but eventually gave in. I could hear the snickers, and the teacher, Mr. Evanson, knew immediately why I had objected. He was very kind and had me come in after school for coaching. His method was to give me a passage in the textbook to memorize and then have me recite it the next day while he corrected my pronunciation. Many years later when I first visited Paris, I knew the layout of the city and many of the famous landmarks that I had memorized years before in *Cours Moyen de Francaise*!

Soon it was Christmas and Aunt Alice gave the three of us twenty dollars to do our Christmas shopping. I had never had that much money to spend on presents, and I found it difficult to find suitable gifts.

Christmas morning was bewildering with so many gifts from the family. Aunt Alice did the Christmas shopping and really went overboard. There were many gifts for each of us. I had been used to one gift only from Mom and one from Aunt Bessie. With all that plenty I felt a bit uncomfortable, but I was especially excited to receive a wristwatch—my first!

At school, as well as the Christmas exams, there was a special assembly where all the students gathered in the auditorium. The programme included *White Christmas*, with the lyrics, "*I'm dreaming of a white Christmas/just like the ones I used to know.*" It brought me to tears. I was a long way from "*where the treetops glisten*" and "*sleigh bells in the snow*" that had been my experience at home.

SPREADING MY WINGS

In June of my first year, students who had a passing mark in their grades could enroll in a programme to go to the country before the school year ended to help farmers whose sons had gone to war. After almost getting down on my knees to beg for the required 50% in chemistry from Mr. Baillie, I was eligible and was sent to Vineland on the Niagara Peninsula.

We crossed Lake Ontario on a passenger ship and were bussed to our camp at Vineland where we were housed in a converted granary down by the water. We were assigned to farmers who picked us up at 8:00 a.m. At Mr. Campbell's we worked till 5, and by that time all the hot water for a shower had been used!

The first crop was rhubarb, which I pulled for eight hours on my first day of work! The next day, I could hardly move. The next crops in succession were strawberries, cherries, peaches, pears and plums. The abundance of fruit to eat was a huge bonus at first, but as the season advanced the novelty was over and before long we ate less. At the end of the season came grapes but by then it was school time and our adventure was over. We paid board—I can't remember the amount but there wasn't much left over as we were paid by piecework. However, I wouldn't have missed the experience for anything as it let me spend my summer in the country, which was the next best thing to being in my old home. And I had escaped the Toronto heat!

CHANGES

That fall of 1943, Iris joined the RCAF, and when she left for training I felt alone. Marjorie had left school and was working; by then we didn't have much in common. I started Grade 12 and though it was hard, I just got on with it. I passed that year though my marks weren't what I had been used to getting. I got a Saturday job as my friends did and that helped the allowance situation. I worked on the produce counter at one of the Power grocery stores in the St. Clair and Bathurst area. It was tiring but lots of fun working with the other Saturday students.

In 1944, I again escaped a Toronto summer! Because I had completed the Royal Life Saving course at school, I was hired by a Toronto boarding school to be a lifeguard for small children and teach them swimming at their camp in cottage country north of Toronto. We travelled to Huntsville in Muskoka to their newly-purchased property that had been a summer camp. I loved being in the country again, especially being north enough to be among spruce and pine trees! It was the closest to being home since leaving two years before. As the train travelled farther north and the conifers became thicker, so did my tears.

Spending most of my time in a bathing suit was a pretty easy way to pass the summer. The children loved the water except they weren't the most enthusiastic of pupils! At the end of the summer I collected my fifty dollars pay!

At Christmas, Iris came home with a boyfriend—an Aussie Air Force fellow. They got engaged and she was supposed to join him in Australia after he was sent back home. He left and she never heard from him again. It must have been hard for her.

That fall I was in Grade 13 and though I did well in some subjects, I struggled in others. Besides, I had taken a job in the shipping department of Langley's, a dry cleaning plant, and worked from four to six o'clock. By the time I'd had dinner, I was pretty tired, but I still had three hours of homework. I now realize what a negative effect that schedule had on my schoolwork, but even though I had more needs at eighteen years old, my allowance was still the same as it was three years before.

Through the years Uncle Stan had talked about the value of higher education, but earlier in the winter when I said I wanted to go to teachers' college after I graduated high school in June, he refused to help me. When I reminded him of what he had promised in his original invitation to live with them, his answer was that if Iris and Marjorie weren't interested in further education he couldn't very well help me. I was stunned but said to myself, *I'll show you*, which I did when he came to my Registered Nurse's graduation five years later!

So here I was in April of Grade 13 and feeling pretty discouraged when Iris was discharged from the air force and returned home. She soon announced that she was moving to Montreal to join a friend and invited me to go with her! I considered this in light of the fact that I was not going to get my year anyhow and that I certainly didn't want to repeat it while living with my Uncle, so I said yes. In those days one could not repeat one subject—the whole year had to be repeated!

Uncle Stan warned me that I needed my Grade 13 and my reply was "I'll get it later," not knowing how or when. I was not dropping out, just postponing it.

MONTREAL

Again, Iris took me under her wing and we arrived in Montreal by train on May 7, 1945, the day before VE Day when the war in Europe ended. Helen, Iris' friend, had rented space in an apartment in a upscale area of Montreal—Notre-Dame-de-Grâce (NDG). It was crowded as the landlady had only one room to rent and she had squeezed three single beds into it, but we felt it could work. And it did.

This new direction in my life was made possible by Iris, and I now wish that I had realized its significance a long time ago. I would have told her so. Iris and I always remained friends, but with time our paths diverged so that we did not share our earlier intimacy. Our time together mostly took the form of family celebrations at Christmas and special occasions. Over the years she had a lot to deal with as she directed whatever form of training there was available for her second son who is developmentally challenged. She also filled the position of church secretary for forty years and made many friends there who are still like family to Tim. When Iris developed Alzheimer's, I drove out of town to see her whenever I could. As the disease progressed, her ability to speak and recognize people waned, but she always became excited when I visited. Our time together was mostly hugs and reminiscing on my part to her.

Thanks, Iris.

In Montreal the next day, Iris and I found our way to the Western Hospital where Aunt Alice's cousin (Aunt? I can't remember her name, but she received us kindly in spite of never having met either of us) was the superintendent of nurses. She gave each of us a job. It was VE Day—victory in Europe—and we were pretty happy!

My job was to receive patients coming into Emergency and to take their history. Some were French speaking only and were generous to this Anglo who had struggled with French at school. On the whole it worked out as we did clinics too. I enjoyed the work, and being with the young nurses in training, most of whom were my age, soon changed my mind about teaching as a vocation. From then on I knew that nursing was my path though I wasn't certain how I would get there. I was missing my Grade 13!

I learned the government had a thank you programme for returning veterans and it was quite a generous one. For every month of service, the veteran was eligible for either a land grant or education plus $60 per month to cover living expenses (it actually did!). Hurray!—I could see a way towards my goal. All I needed to take advantage of the programme was to be a veteran!!

I soon learned the government was recruiting for the war in the Pacific, so on my eighteenth birthday—June 21, 1945—I was first in line at the recruitment centre. I left as Private Butt, No 40853 in the Canadian Women's' Army Corps (CWAC) and I was on my way! Not very patriotic but certainly practical!

ARMY LIFE

I was posted to the Saint Sulpice barracks for new recruits in downtown Montreal where I received an armload of new clothes—my army uniform! The CWAC was known to have the smartest uniform of all the services as it had been designed by a Paris designer. It fit me perfectly, and I wore it proudly.

Within a week or so we were on our way to Kitchener, Ontario, where we received our basic training, which consisted mostly of learning to march in the July heat! This was also where I received my first vaccination. A couple of days later I had a raging fever and a very sore arm. If this was caused by only one pustule I can only imagine the suffering if one actually had a case of smallpox!

Six weeks later I was posted to Woodstock, (Ontario, that is!), and I took up the job of sick bay attendant, which was a breeze with lots of free time as there was seldom anyone in the two-bed room! My previous hospital work experience was in my record, so when I was given the choice of sick bay or office work, I chose the one that would allow me to move around. Sitting all day behind a desk didn't appeal to me.

After several months I was posted to London, Ontario, and before long the war in the Pacific was over on August 16, 1945. We all went downtown to join the jubilant crowds—singing, shouting, kissing and dancing. It was memorable!

I was discharged there in early September and was again a civilian back in Toronto at Uncle Stan's and Aunt Alice's.

THE NEXT STEP

By now Iris was working in the principal's office at the Training and Re-establishment Institute Toronto (TRIT). Veterans called it rehab, and it was the government's answer to the hordes of veterans newly discharged and needing training for jobs or further education. Mostly it was training in the trades, but it also taught Grade 13. After the flood of veterans was over, it became Ryerson Technical and many years later, Ryerson University. Those vets who were university bound had to complete their Grade 13 before September in order to begin their studies at the University of Toronto. Those men had been high school students who, on reaching their eighteenth birthday, had been conscripted into one of the three services. Now the government was offering the lucky ones who made it home a way to continue their education. These new students who flooded the University of Toronto that year were now mostly men and very motivated. My male neighbours in their 90s here at Christie Gardens, the retirement residence where I live, could have been in that class!

It was a way for me to finish my schooling, which I needed to advance to further education. So, I began my second attempt at Grade 13 in April 1946.

Taught mostly by retired teachers, we crammed a much condensed version of Grade 13 into four months and graduated with the coveted diploma in August. My marks were OK, but one stood out close to the end of the course: geometry. Mr. Jackson, my Analytical Geometry teacher at Oakwood, wrote the textbook. He had been very strict on following the logical steps in solving a theorem, and I must have absorbed his method well because I got 100% on the last test that summer at the veteran's school. The teacher handed back each student's paper after announcing the name and mark. Mine was the last and he called out my name without the mark, so I was sure I had failed. Everybody was looking my way as he passed it back upside down, and I thought I had failed too miserably for him to announce my mark. I had scored 100%! Why had he treated me differently? Could it be in that roomful of men (except for one other female) that he didn't want to embarrass them? Or maybe he felt I had cheated and my mark didn't count? How does one cheat in geometry? I'll never know as I didn't have the confidence to ask him.

I finally had my long-delayed Grade 13, which could open the door to whichever higher education I chose. However, I had no money—army pay had been pretty low, and it was next to impossible to save anything, so my next step was to find a job!

I approached the Bell Telephone Company and was taken on as a potential long distance operator. After a short training in the intricacies of putting through a long distance call—and after learning all the abbreviations for the major cities and towns in North America—we learned how, as operators, to connect people to their desired numbers by plugging in a long cord to the board and physically timing their calls. There was no such thing as dialing one's own long distance calls for another twenty-five or thirty years. I still remember the abbreviations over seventy years later!

After almost a year as a long distance operator, I was ready for something more active and took a job with the Toronto Golf Club as a waitress for the summer. We lived in and had one day off a week. While at the golf club I saved some money, which together with my earlier savings I thought would see me through the three years of nurse's training. I applied and was accepted at Wellesley Hospital for the September class.

I had considered the university nursing course but that would have involved finding a place to live and feeding myself after the twelve months of veteran's benefits that I was entitled to ran out. I just didn't have the funds for that! There was a proviso to the university programme that a student's $60 per month plus tuition would continue if their marks were in the top third of the class. My confidence in achieving this wasn't great considering my high school experience, so I chose the more secure route. At Wellesley Hospital the students were assured of room and board for the three years and that gave me the security I needed.

NURSING EDUCATION

Hospital Nursing Education was considered second to none as it combined classroom lectures with practical experience on the floors. By the time we graduated, we'd had three years' experience and could run a floor. As for marks, I always stood either second or third in a class of thirty-five, so my confidence in academics took a step forward!

On the practical side, costs were always one of the first considerations as my budget was pretty tight and allowed for no frills—I even had to think twice about the occasional chocolate bar! I still have the little notebook in which I wrote every purchase. I managed to budget for my cigarettes—I smoked a half at a time! I rolled my own on a V-Master arrangement that rolled one long cigarette that I then cut into five regular length cigarettes with a scalpel! It hadn't been easy learning how to smoke—I had given up once and started again because all the cool people smoked, and being a veteran I thought I was pretty cool!

There were some outlays at first for uniforms and equipment that I hadn't expected so that crimped me further. Toward the end of my third year when funds were running out, Aunt Alice gave me back my board money that I had paid her when I was working. So generous and a godsend! I think Iris had put out the word because Uncle Stan paid for my graduation dress. $40 for a fancy dress was average in 1950! This was the first new outfit I had during my three years of training.

For our yearly big dance, I had made my outfits as I did all my other clothes. I bought the most fashionable patterns, so my clothes didn't look amateurish. Following the directions in the pattern was the way that I learned to sew!

Another item that stretched my budget was stockings. Nylons had just replaced silk or lisle (cotton) and were just as sheer as silk and stronger. However, they did develop runs—a disaster on my budget—and I bought a special tiny ratchet hooking device that made the run disappear as I hooked up the run strand by strand; it was labour-intensive but effective! Pantyhose came later and garter belts disappeared, at least for everyday wear!

At that time all nurses were trained at hospitals under the apprenticeship system where students learned through a combination of lectures and hands-on procedures. As we became proficient we were assigned, under supervision, to patients on the floor so it worked out very well. Most of us were fresh out of school teenage girls who, it was hoped, wouldn't kill anybody! Sometimes mistakes did occur.

I made my only mistake when I gave a fresh post-operative man with a colostomy a laxative rather than a painkiller! The medicine cups had moved on the squared paper sheet and the name squares were no longer accurate. I was called down to the nursing office where I was given a talking to. Whew, not dismissed! I changed my system of delivering medications! The patient's doctor wrote an order for the nurse who had given his patient the laxative pills to take two herself that night! The patient survived but had a busy night!

VANCOUVER AND LEN

After a year or so of doing private duty in Toronto after graduation, I moved to Vancouver. I had fantasized as a student in Clarke's Beach about going there some day when I could see Newfoundland on one corner of the continent and Vancouver on the other. Maps have always fascinated me and as a much younger child in St. George's, I would amuse myself by drawing the map of Newfoundland from memory!

The opportunity came when friends were being moved to Vancouver and invited me to drive out with them. Ivy and Norman Armstrong were from Vancouver and for them it meant they were returning home. It was the beginning of a whole new life for me!

I knew no one except the Armstrongs, but that didn't matter. I was in a beautiful city full of spring flowers—even the trees were in bloom in April—and I soon had a job! In those days a nurse would only have to turn up at the nursing office of a hospital and she would have a job! My rented room at 14th and Cambie was within walking distance of the Vancouver General Hospital—the largest in Canada at that time with 1200 beds. I was assigned to a surgical floor where I soon made friends. I loved it.

And I soon had a boyfriend. In July, there was a big changeover when the new junior interns started, and one of them asked me out. My next move was to go on permanent nights so I could have more beach time! I would get off my night shift at eight in the morning, sleep till 1:00 p.m. and have the rest of the long day free. On one of my days off the fellow I was going with called in sick so we could go to the beach. Being fair-skinned, he turned up for work the next day with a very obvious sunburn. It wasn't hard to tell he hadn't been sick the day before, and I kept my mouth shut!

About the same time, a friend at work, BJ Lyle, introduced me to Len, my future husband. Shortly after starting at the Vancouver General I had recognized her cap as being from the Hospital for Sick Children in Toronto and I spoke to her. We met frequently at coffee break and on returning from her holidays a couple of weeks later, she told me she was engaged and said to me, "Bob's got the cutest roommate—we've got to get you two together." That sounded interesting, so she arranged a picnic at Boundary Bay. I had worked until seven that morning, gone to bed around eight after breakfast and was fast asleep at eleven a.m. when BJ shook me awake. The guys were waiting in the car and off we went, Len and I in the back seat. On three hours' sleep I couldn't have been a very interesting companion, and I found him rather quiet. At Boundary Bay the boys rented a boat and rowed out to a small island where some of us swam but not me—the water was icy.

However, the picnic was a success I guess as he called me in a few days and invited me to a movie. When I pulled out my glasses at the movie, he exclaimed "YOU WEAR GLASSES!" and that was all. He usually spoke his mind directly! Typically, I didn't pursue his comment. I think I had a fear of getting into an argument because I wasn't good at confrontation. It wasn't in my background. Apart from that we had a lovely evening and he certainly cut an impressive figure in his well-cut suit and tie—all dressed up and certainly the handsomest man I had ever gone out with. His car was also noticeable. Because he worked for Coca-Cola, he drove a RED car with those very words covering both sides. We were easily identified!

It was only after a few more dates that he asked me if he could kiss me. ASKED! I was impressed and after that kiss, I was hooked. He was a gentleman and was considerate, but it was not my heart but my head that ruled my decisions. We dated all fall and one evening after pub-crawling with a group of friends he asked me to marry him. I was surprised and my answer was "Ask me again when you've not been drinking!" I certainly wasn't going to commit to a life-altering arrangement with someone I had gone out with only intermittently for a few months. I felt I needed more time to get to know him better.

Besides, I was getting the feeling he was taking me for granted. When he travelled for business he didn't let me know but expected me to be available when he got back to town. Once, when he and friends were planning a get-together for a visiting friend from Toronto, he said he would pick me up at a certain time. I said I was busy when I wasn't. It was the first I had heard of it and thought, "If this guy thinks I'm just waiting around for him to call, it's time I sent him a message." It must have annoyed him because it was weeks before I saw him again at a party. BJ again played Cupid and arranged a party that we both attended! I hadn't heard from him all summer and we barely acknowledged each other all evening. When it was time to leave, he asked if he could drive me home. He told me that his summer had been hectic with his grandfather dying in Toronto, his going back for the funeral and the death of his grandmother shortly after. They had been an important part of his life.

Years later after we were married, Len told me that while spending time with his grandmother after the funeral, she said that at twenty-five years old, it was time for him find a wife! We dated for the rest of the fall and he always asked for a date before going out of town!

On New Year's Eve he again asked me to marry him and the answer was the same: that I didn't know him well enough. He left for Toronto the next day for a business meeting and rather than returning to Vancouver at the end of the week, he resigned from Coca-Cola and joined his father in his candy business. He wasn't coming back!

So, a long distance romance by mail started. We both wrote twice a week and I must confess I waited eagerly for those letters for they were full of love and entreaties to come back east. I was really torn for I loved Vancouver—the city, the climate, the variety of flowers and foliage, the sea. I also had Aunt Maud and Uncle Will (Aunt Bessie and Uncle Jim's relatives) who lived there, and their place was my second home. Also, several Wellesley classmates were now living in Vancouver and Victoria, so I had lots of reasons to stay. However, I decided to go back east to get to know this man who had become very interesting to me. I left Vancouver in the middle of March.

RETURNING EAST

Getting to know Len better and meeting his lovely, warm family helped me make up my mind. On my birthday—June 21—he arrived with a ring and an eager look on his face! It was mid-morning and I was in my dressing gown ironing a uniform before going on duty. I still hadn't given him an answer, but I accepted the ring and have worn it proudly for sixty-eight years.

I saved like crazy for the wedding as I was determined to have one as nice as those of my friends. It wasn't easy as I had no offer of help from my uncle. This meant the number of invitations had to be limited, which turned out to be especially difficult for Len's family. Foolishly, I didn't tell Len and his family the reason for the budget because pride got in the way.

We were married on October 16, 1952, in St. George's United Church in Toronto. And then we really started to get to know each other! Often these days, a couple live together while travelling this sometimes rocky path, but in our day, in our circles, that wasn't done. But we survived and forged a new path together as we found ways of understanding each other.

Len had a significant loss at an early age that had always been painful for him. When Len's father, whose work took him away all week, discovered that his wife was having an affair with the next door neighbour, he took Len and moved to his parents' home. An acrimonious divorce followed that gave his father sole custody and no visiting rights for his mother. In 1929 divorce was a scandal and a decision like this was possible! For Len, it was as though his mother had died, for she was lost to him—a terrible blow at four years old. The separation was made even more painful when he was told by his grandmother that his mother was a bad woman who didn't love him anymore and that Len wasn't to ask about her. In those days, people thought children would forget!

The years went by with this painful wound always present for him until one day, in his fiftieth year, his Aunt Violet mentioned that she had seen a death notice for his mother's husband (the same man) in a Toronto paper. She also told Len she had LIKED HIS MOTHER! This was the first time he had ever heard anything positive about his mother and this helped him decide to get in touch with her. This was a huge step for Len as he had always believed his mother didn't want him, and he hadn't risked being rejected twice.

When our first child was born, Len's father had offered to put him in touch with his mother through her brother, Uncle William, but Len was still too fragile to attempt it then. Now he was ready. When approached, Uncle William was very kind and welcoming and offered to pass on Len's telephone number to his mother. Len waited two excruciating days with no phone call and on the third day called her number from his office downtown. When she answered, he told her who he was and asked if he could come to see her. She replied "Of course." He left work, tore uptown the two miles to where she lived and was reunited after forty-six years!

It was an emotional reunion for them both. She pulled out his first shoes and his favourite toy from the bottom drawer in her bedroom. He now had proof that his mother had not rejected him, and that the separation had been imposed on them both. She was a lovely lady, was happy to know her grandchildren and remained an important part of our family until she died several years later.

The job with Len's father didn't work out. He and his partner were in the candy manufacturing business and they wanted someone to represent their business on the road. Though Len was able to generate some sales, they weren't enough to support an extra person and regretfully Len resigned. Everyone was sad. By then I was pregnant with Paul and no longer eligible for private duty work, the only area available to me, so Len needed to change jobs.

He was soon offered two jobs, one of which would have required us to move out of town, so he took the one that was Toronto based—IBM. Neither of us had heard of IBM as it wasn't well known in Toronto in 1953. Not only that, Len knew nothing about business machines and when he asked during his initial interview what the remuneration would be he was told that if he couldn't take $6000 a year, IBM didn't want him! That was a pretty exciting figure to us as we had both been earning the usual $2000 a year!

IBM was good to us. Those who did well and reached the top rung were sent together with their wives, to the Golden Circle conference. Len qualified for many of these awards and we had some wonderful travel experiences. Among them were trips to Mexico City, Singapore, Hawaii and Paris. At that time IBM was riding high with their electric typewriters and other office products and was very generous. In Paris, the Eiffel Tower restaurant closed at lunch-time in order to host an IBM lunch! When the event was in Singapore, instead of flying there over the Pacific, we changed our tickets to travel first to Frankfurt then on to India, Nepal and Sri Lanka before Singapore.

In India we met people whom I had written to before leaving Toronto. They subscribed to the same small publication that we did that emphasized positive ways of living. Some became friends. I'd had no reply from any of them before leaving home because our letters had crossed, and we had no way of knowing whether they would be interested in meeting us! As we were having a late breakfast on our first morning in Delhi, the phone rang in the hotel dining room and we were approached by the waiter who asked if we were the Tyrrells! It was Gopal Kulkarni, a subscriber to whom I had written before leaving Toronto, who was phoning all the hotels to find out where we might be staying! We remained in touch for many years.

We never made reservations anywhere on our trips, we liked to take our chances! All the way through India—Calcutta, Agra, Varanasi—we were treated with great kindness. At Varanasi where devotees come to the Ganges at dawn, we saw people bathe in the water, drink it, and a little farther along, sweep the ashes of a funeral pyre into it! Unforgettable.

Tourists are swamped by people wanting them to buy wares and services, and we finally succumbed to a boat ride. As we gained some distance from the shore and joined the many boats there, Len, after much gesturing with the boatman, changed places with him and rowed along with all the others. Our boatman sat behind Len and took a ribbing from his fellows who were convulsed with laughter. It was an unbelievable and unforgettable sight. Len loved boats and the water, and his salesman skills got him a memorable experience!

By the time we arrived in Singapore for the conference, Len was really sick with Dengue Fever. We had been in Nepal where he was bitten by a mosquito. He had to miss most of the conference and lost a lot of weight. When the conference was over, he needed time to recover so I had to find a hotel we could afford. I was told there was an old hotel up the road, and when I went to check it out found myself at the famous Raffles! The rooms were on the second floor and were reached by an old Victorian central staircase. One room had Somerset Maugham's name on the door. Guess it was permanently reserved! It was here that Len recovered and where we met Hettie.

Down at the end of the little alley just outside Raffles there was a "sale" sign in a small shop that I thought I should check out. The sales-person who was helping out her friend, the owner, was in only for that day. She took me for an American, but when I told her I was a Canadian, she said she was from Vancouver! As I had lived there, we chatted about that but it wasn't until I was leaving that she said she was from Newfoundland! Wow! The door closed and we talked some more! We compared places where we had lived and eventually found she was from the same small village as my grandmother who was from Port de Grave in Conception Bay on the east coast! We couldn't believe it when she disclosed she had the same last name as my grandmother: "Dawe." At that time, Port de Grave was a tiny fishing village of probably less than 100 people with half of them having the name "Dawe." We decided to be cousins! She entertained us in her home in Singapore and we remained friends until her death some years later.

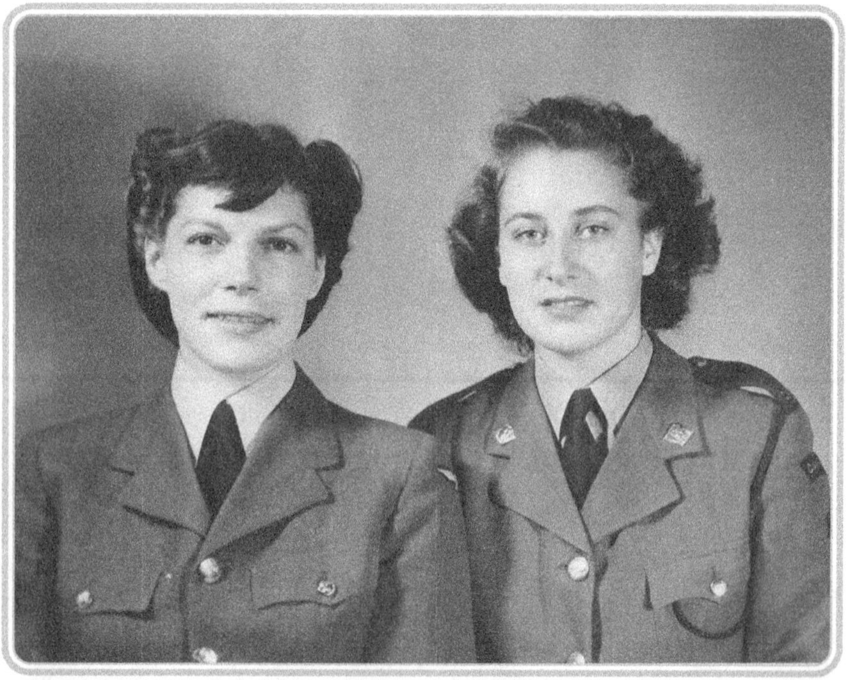

Cavell and Iris RCAF, ARMY

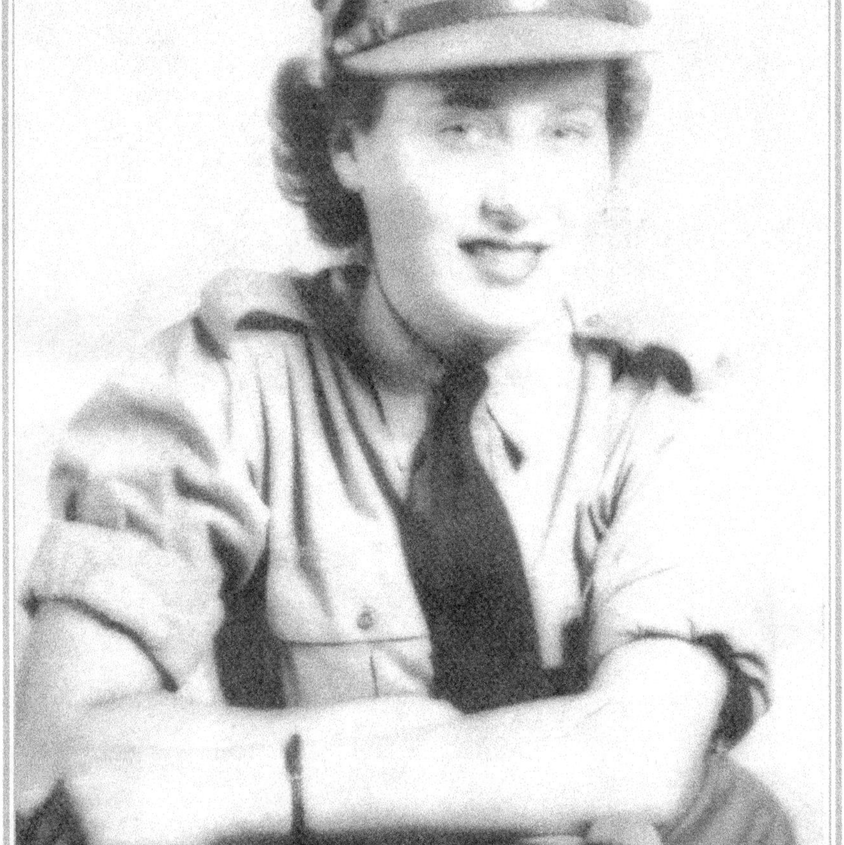

Cavell - Army 1945

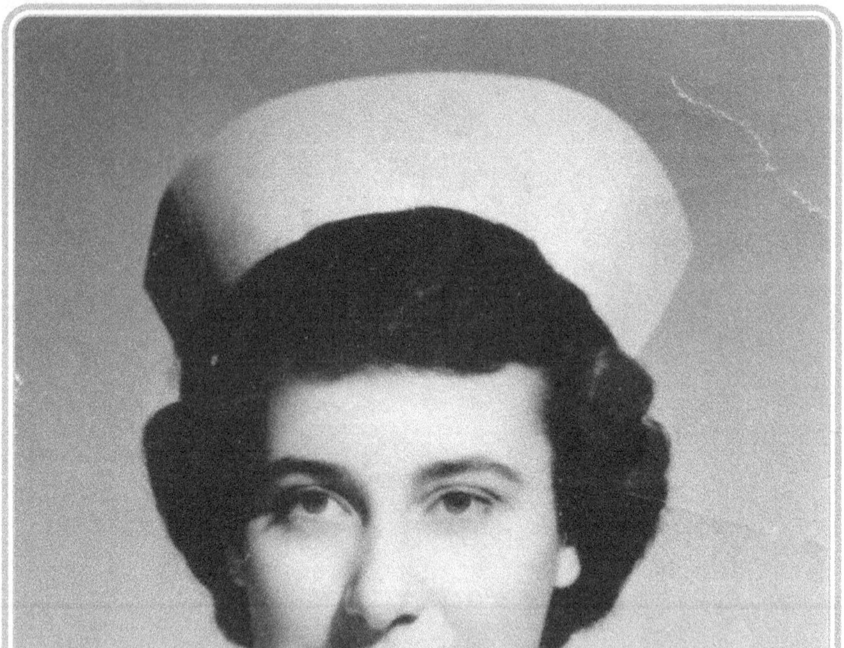

Cavell - nurse 1950

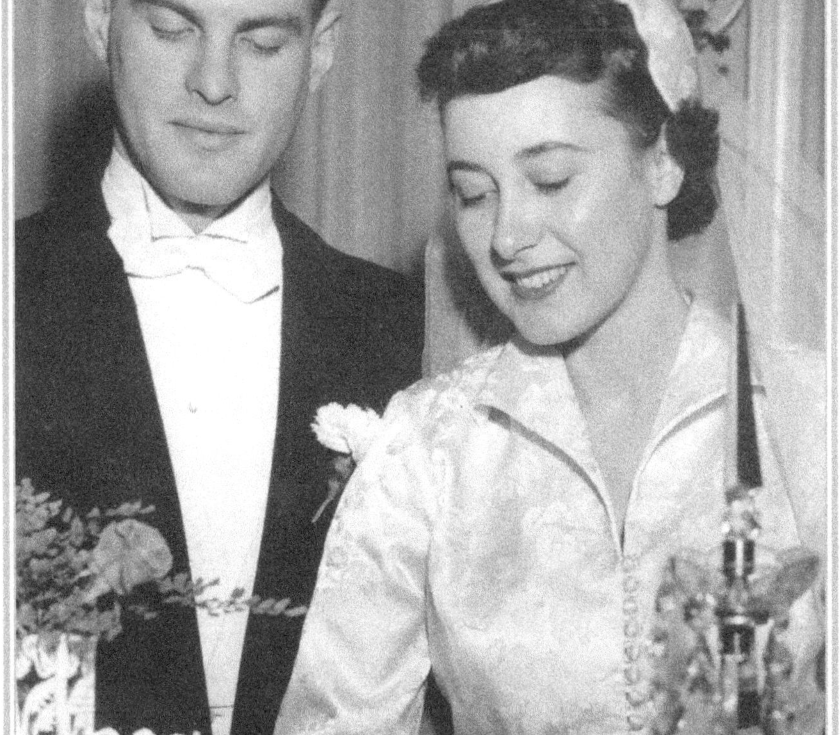

Wedding Len and Cavell's wedding 1952

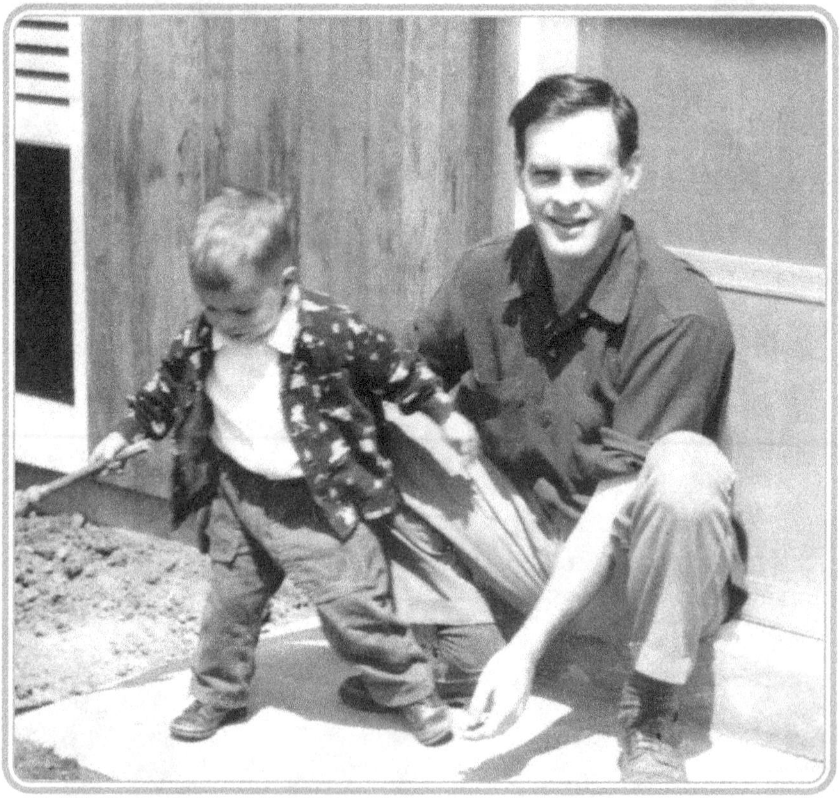

Len and Paul 1956

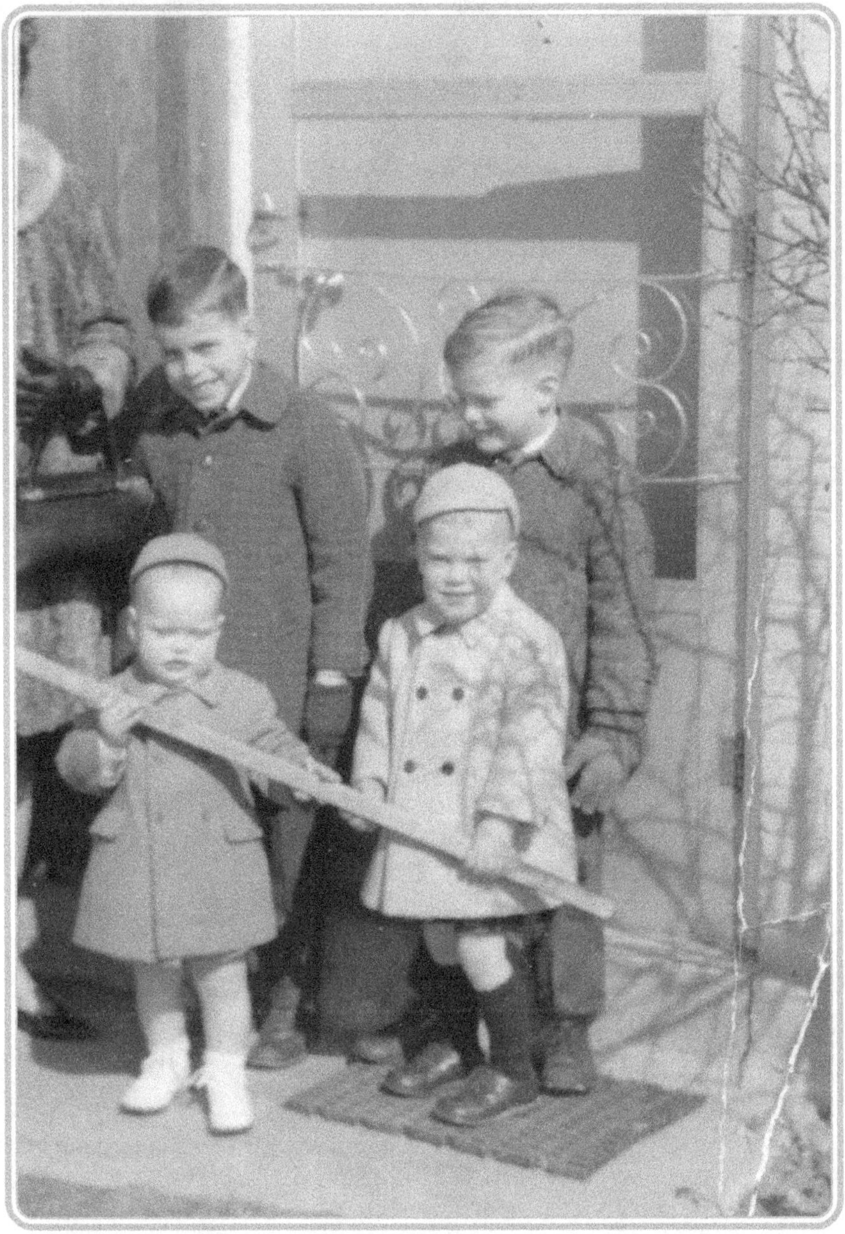

Four boys 1963

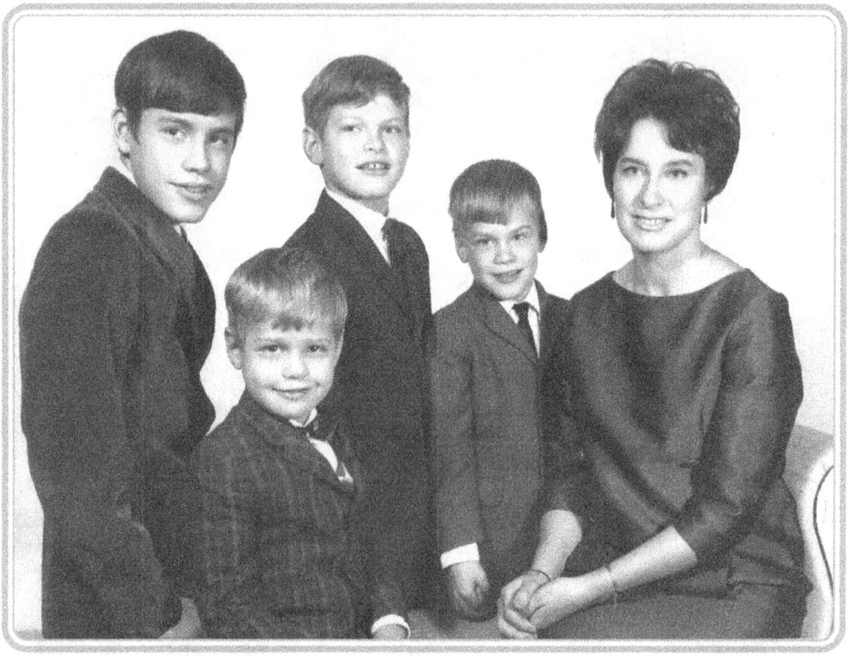

Cavell and four boys - Ottawa 1967

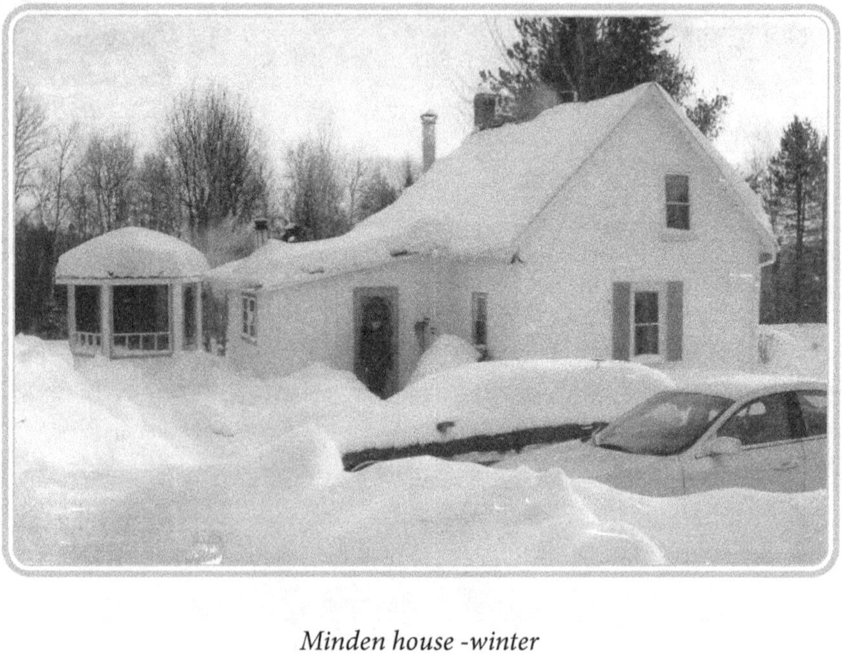

Minden house -winter

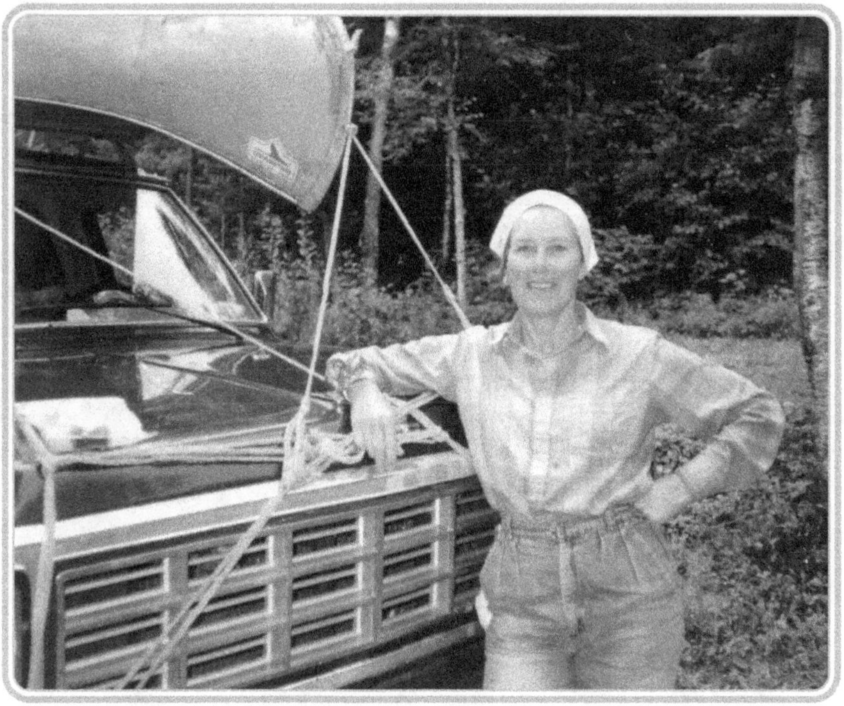

Cavell, Nfld canoe trip

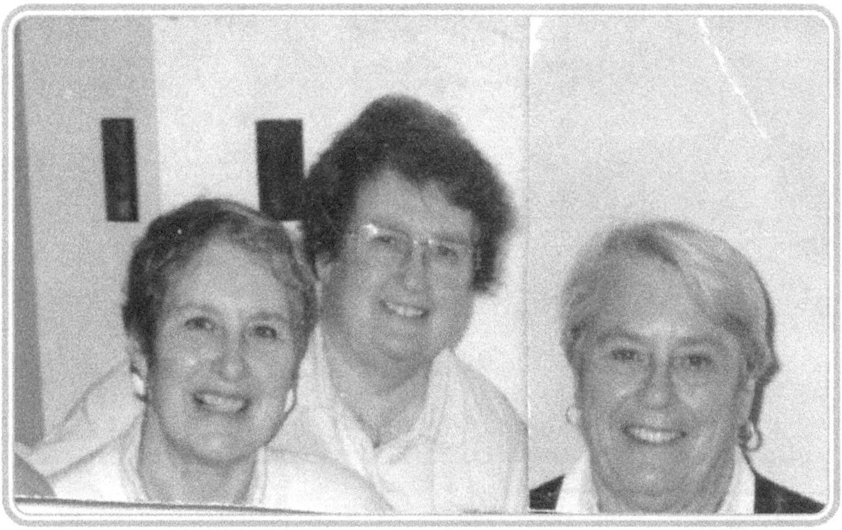

Three sisters, Cavell, Shirley, Phyllis, 1990s

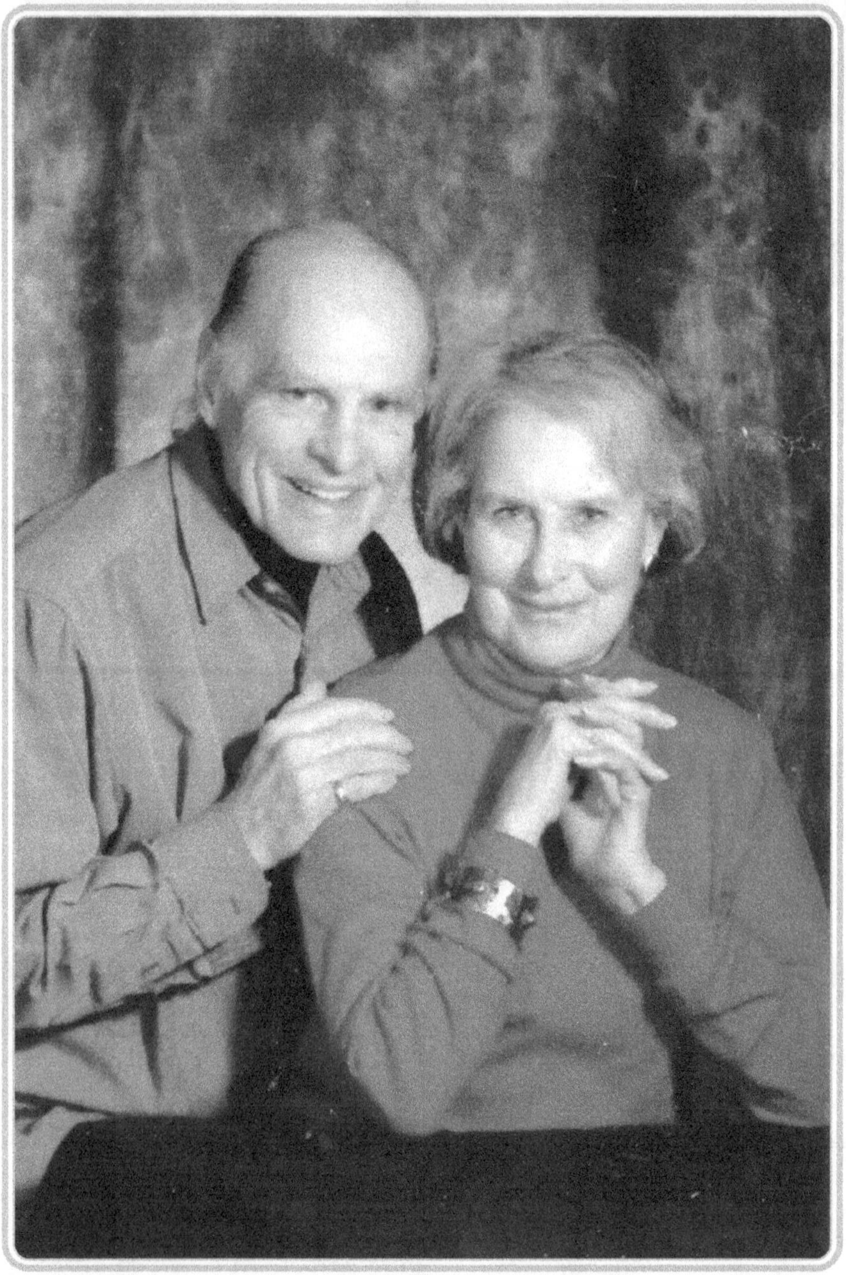

Cavell and Len portrait

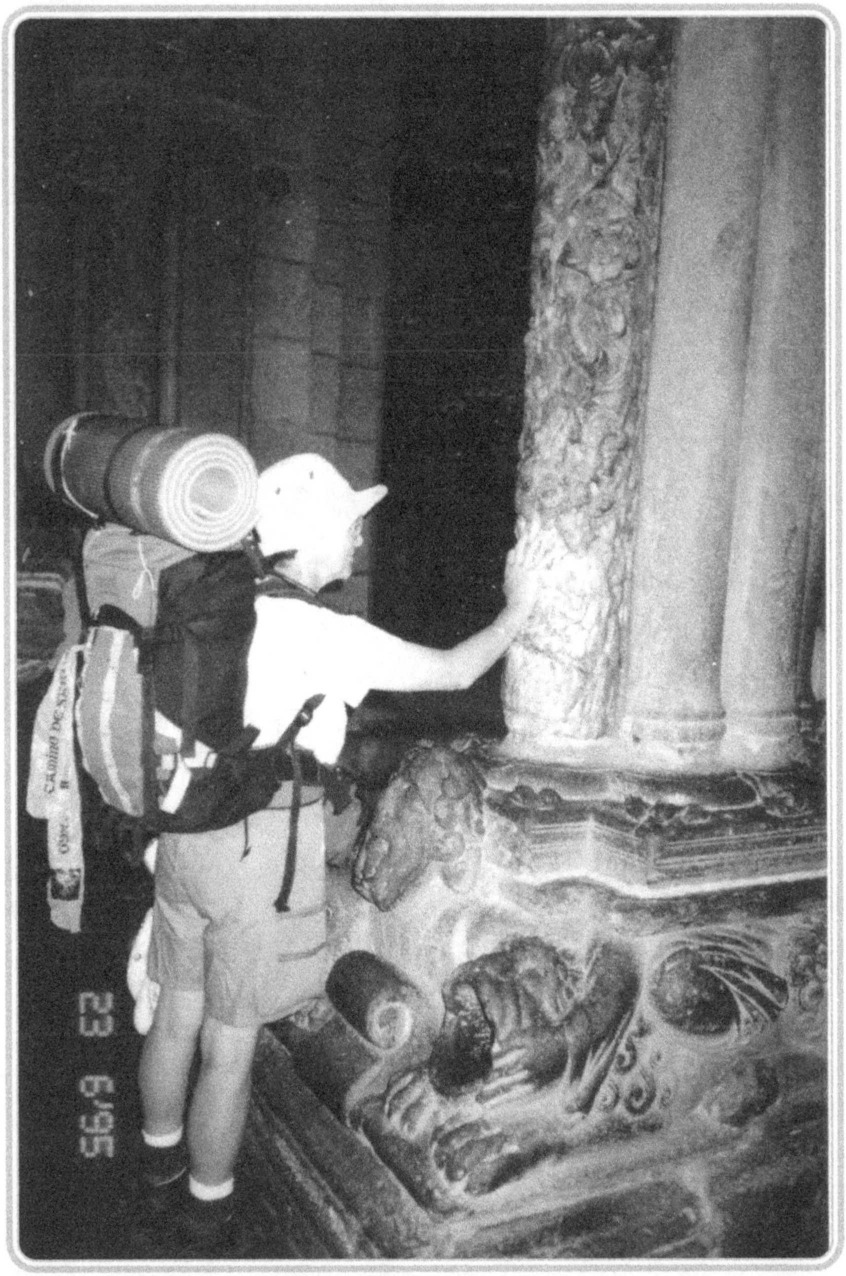

Cavell at Santiago Cathedral

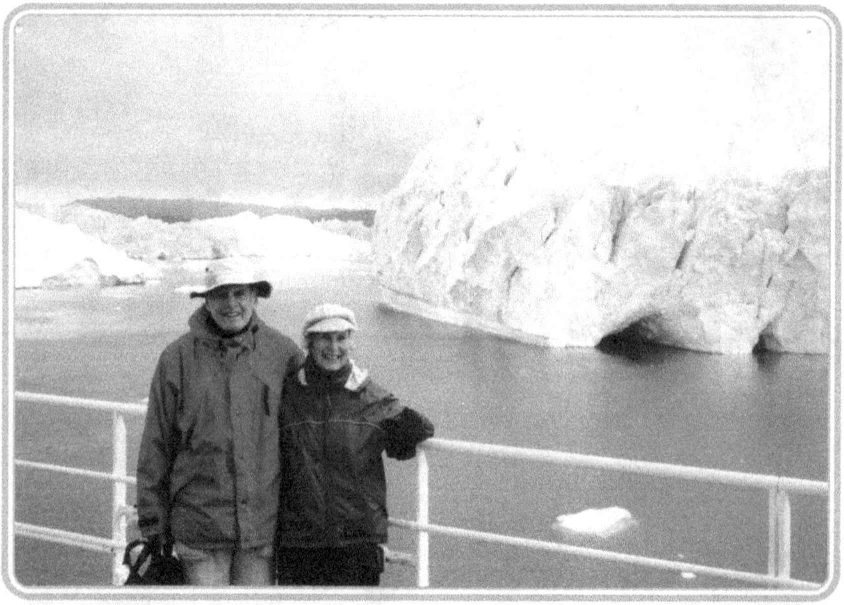

Len and Cavell 50th anniversary. - Disco Bay, Arctic.

BACK TO THE 50S

Now I return to the fifties and to my new life with Len.

Just a little more than thirteen months after our marriage, Paul was born on November 24, 1953. He was followed by David on August 30, 1956; Christopher on June 28, 1960; and Edward (Ted) on September 27, 1961. We had a lively household and I loved being the mother of boys. I had come from a female household—a grandmother, a mother and two sisters—even the cat was female! I loved the boys' energy, their readiness for anything and their forthrightness. We were a great household!

Paul was a sweet little guy who didn't seek the limelight but loved to trail his father everywhere. He was good to his little brothers when they came along, showing them the ropes when it came to skating in the backyard and camping.

David was a wonderful older brother to the younger ones—kind and loving and a wrestling partner for Paul. Often in the evening after homework, we would hear the thump, thump coming from the third floor as they developed teenage muscles!

The younger two were almost like a second family coming four years after David and just fifteen months apart. Chris would comfort Ted when he was little by saying with wide open arms, "Come to me Teddy" whereupon Ted would run to him to be held. As they grew older, however,

Ted learned that Chris had buttons that could be pushed, which made for some lively times!

When Ted was thirty he found out that a weak knee was actually Multiple Sclerosis. At this point in 2020 he has lived with it for almost thirty years and it has taken an awful toll. He can't move, swallow or speak, but earlier, when he could, he replied to my question "What keeps you going?" by answering "Life has too much to offer!" What an attitude!

His daughter, Alexa, means so much to him but her living in Peterborough does not allow for as much time together as they would like. He is still in his own apartment with twenty-four hour care, and Christopher shares a lot of the oversight needed. Thank goodness for the Ontario Health Care system that takes care of most of the cost.

Acting was part of David's life from an early age when he had parts in commercials and later in middle school and high school productions. At fifteen, he had a professional part in a production of *Galileo* in a large downtown theatre. Close to his graduation from Grade 13, he accepted a part in *A Streetcar Named Desire* in the same theatre, but just as rehearsals were starting he began having trouble with his memory. By June, I began to see a change in his persona. Some days he was more easily angered, which wasn't like him and often his expression was different. I didn't understand it but being either naive or unwilling to deal with something like drugs that I didn't understand, I let it go. My way was to give teenagers the space they needed to work things out.

One day David announced at suppertime that he had been knocked out when a car had run into him, knocking him off on his bike. The driver had taken him to the hospital and then driven him home. Little was made of concussions in those days but immediately he had trouble studying for his exams and memorizing his lines for the play. Our family doctor sent David to a psychiatrist who diagnosed schizophrenia. Later, bipolar was added. Neither of the doctors were aware that part of the picture was most likely a concussion and some drug use. In any case, the seriousness of concussions was not as well understood in the seventies as it is now.

And it went on from there. David was in and out of hospital and on different drugs for four years until he took his own life. This family disaster affected us all. We were all wounded.

We accepted family counselling at home, though neither Christopher nor Ted would take part. Paul was by then living with friends and working after university. They didn't want to relive any of it. It was how we all felt, for we didn't talk about the horrible event even though it coloured our everyday life. Many years later from a more knowledgeable place I know that we should have had more professional help during the process and afterwards. Hindsight is great. Even today I still fight the "should haves" and the "what ifs."

In the fall of '75 after Grandma Dolly died, Len's Dad, Grandpa Gordon, came to live with us, returning to the home of his youth. He was a lovely man, appreciative of being with us and later on of everything being done for him as his health declined. The death of David, to whom he had been close, was an enormous shock to him and, I think, hastened his decline.

Len's grandparents had been looked after latterly by their daughter, Auntie Winnie Nelson, and when they died she and her husband, Uncle Wesley, bought the house, 100 Stibbard, from the estate. When they finished bringing up their own family there and were ready for a smaller place, they sold it to us in 1963 when we were bursting at the seams in our small bungalow in Don Mills. It was a great house for a family, with lots of rooms on three floors and a finished basement for young boys to play games, including pool, with their friends. By the time our own grandchildren came along, there had been five generations of Tyrrells in that house. It was in the Tyrrell family from 1920 to 2007 when we sold it and moved to Christie Gardens, a retirement facility.

Meanwhile, my two younger sisters grew up, had careers and families. Phyllis, who went to St. John's after high school to work in Aunt Bessie's store, left after a couple of years to begin nurse's training. She came to Toronto and eventually moved to Vancouver where she met her husband, Murray Einarson, and had a daughter and a son—Patty and Murray.

Murray senior was in the Canadian Air Force, and when he was discharged a couple of years later, they moved to Silicon Valley in California where he worked at Hewlett-Packard while Phyllis nursed at Stanford Hospital.

My younger sister, Shirley, became a teacher, marrying Bob Squires after a year of teaching in St. George's. They had three daughters, Judy, Carol and Debbie, and moved to Labrador City where Shirley became a well-loved English teacher.

My sisters and I kept our connection by letter-writing in our youth, but once we had families of our own it became even more important to us that our children get to know each other.

Phyllis was the sister who put the most effort into getting us together. One year, Murray surprised her with a convertible to replace her ageing car. In July, she packed her two children into the car along with sandwich makings and drinks, clamped her knitted peaked cap on her head and took off for Toronto 2700 miles away. With the children taking turns as navigators and sandwich makers, they made it to Toronto in three days! She insisted that she hadn't driven fast, but "fast" is subjective! She did say that no time was spent at stops other than for gas and toilet trips!

Phyllis, Murray and Patty drove from California to Toronto twice, rested for a couple of days, then piled into my wagon with my four children to drive to Newfoundland where we met Shirley and her three girls. They had driven over 1000 miles from the interior of Labrador to meet us. We camped and sang the Newfoundland folk songs of which Phyllis, especially, knew all the words.

This was our way of joining the family together again, and the cousins got to know each other. Now in their sixties, they still keep in touch and visit each other. They feel their family connection and roots. Their grandparents would be pleased. It would have broken their hearts to see my sisters and me split up as children.

After our parents died and we went to live with various relatives, we gradually got used to the loneliness and separation. At least, I did. We all lived hundreds of miles apart, and my sisters' lives became very separate from mine, which in time seemed quite normal. It was Phyllis, who after moving to California, began the process that in time developed into the strong bond that still endures. In the days before long distance telephoning was a fact of life, Phyllis, encouraged by Murray, used to call occasionally. At that time long distance was prohibitively expensive and the normal mode of communication was by letter. I really looked forward to those letters and in time we talked regularly and became much closer. We shared our lives to a much greater degree than when we were growing up.

Whenever there was a family crisis or illness, Phyllis and Shirley were on the next plane, as was I. After Phyllis died, Shirley and I continued this. We all shared a solid, caring relationship and have Phyllis to thank for seeding it.

Phyllis had a lot to forgive me for over the years, but she continued to love me. I didn't realize how much until after she died. There were many incidents of thoughtless action as I wrestled with my own demons, but we never became bad friends over these incidents as sometimes happens in families. I credit this to Phyllis' forgiving nature, and I appreciate it more than words can say. I wish I could tell her now. She was the sister most responsible for the closeness we enjoyed as adults and the closeness between all our children and now their children. What a gift!

Aunt Bessie always accommodated us and our families both in St. John's and at her place on Hodgewater Line in the country. She generously filled a big gap for all of us. When she was in her eighties Phyllis and I took turns having Aunt Bessie for the winter, which she really enjoyed. She was a gregarious person, enjoyed life and fitted in wherever she was. In Toronto, she and her childhood friends who had come to Toronto in their twenties and who had always kept in touch were again like schoolgirls when they got together! The stories and laughter flowed. When Aunt Bessie went to stay with each of them for a few days, her gift was a Scrabble game complete with a wordbook, which she taught them all to play. Her teacher experience never left her!

My own family has grown with grandchildren. Paul was the first to marry and lives in Burlington, Ontario. He and his wife, Ann, have two daughters: Nicole and Laura. He is a grandfather to Nicole and Pete's baby, Isla. They live in San Francisco.

Christopher has one son, Ben, and is divorced from Mardi. They all live in Toronto, and Chris and Mardie remain friends and share family get-togethers.

Ted is divorced from Beverly and has one daughter, Alexa, who lives in Peterborough. That is how Len and I, the parents of boys, got our girls!

As for our own family, in 1965, Len was promoted to manager of the IBM office products in Ottawa, and we moved there in June. We rented a large old farmhouse on the western edge of Ottawa. This was a great place to live as behind the house was a long hill where the boys sledded in winter, a large front lawn with a tree-house, and behind, a huge hedge of lilacs that gave off a wonderful scent in spring. The house overlooked the Ottawa river and Britannia Beach with its sailing club, so we almost felt like we were on vacation year round! Being on the heights we experienced the intense weather that barrelled down the long Ottawa Valley—exciting at times with the wind and rain!

Although Ottawa is known to be one of the two coldest capitals in the world (the other being Moscow), we were determined to enjoy it and joined a ski club on the Quebec side of the Ottawa River in the Gatineau region. It was a short drive over the bridge to the unspoiled hills of the Laurentians, and our boys and Len enjoyed their winter fun. Mother struggled as she was an adult learner!

It was a good time to be living in Ottawa as it was Canada's 100th birthday in 1967 and the schools took children to many significant sites. It was a great way to learn about our nation's history and its capital.

On the very cold New Year's Eve of 1967, Canada's 100th birthday, we, along with our friends the Stirlings, stood on Parliament Hill at midnight to watch Prime Minister Lester Pearson light the new everlasting flame.

It was a memorable event and whenever I see that flame fifty years later on TV, I remember that night! Afterwards we took our freezing bodies back to our friends' house for hot cocoa!

I made another close friend while living in Ottawa. We lived on a busy highway, but across the road was a cul-de-sac of new housing. There I met and became a longtime friend of Naomi Jackson Groves when we discovered a mutual love of Temagami! She was, among other pursuits, a painter following in the footsteps of her Group of Seven uncle, AY Jackson, who at that time lived in Ottawa.

Her home was filled with her uncle's art and when I inquired if it were possible to buy one his sketches, she brought out a pile of them from her bedroom closet! When she looked them over, she pronounced them as being "not that great" and asked me to wait until the end of summer when AY would be returning from a sketching trip to Georgian Bay. When he was back in town and she still hadn't seen his summer sketches, she said it would be better if I went downtown to his apartment to look them over and gave me his phone number. When I called, he said, "Sure," and welcomed me warmly. I picked out a sketch from his pile titled *Morse Island, Georgian Bay*, which we have enjoyed.

A few years later as AY's health diminished, the McMichaels, who had established a gallery of Group of Seven art in Kleinburg, near Toronto, invited AY to live with them. He had a favourite corner at the gallery where he held court daily, talking to visitors. Once, he and his aid came to lunch at 100 Stibbard, and our boys all made sure they came home from school to join us.

In the late fall of 1967, a family who had been our neighbours in Don Mills stayed with us while they searched for a house in Ottawa. The mother coughed a lot and a couple of months later we received a notice from the health department advising us to get chest x-rays as our friend had been diagnosed with TB! Everybody in our family was negative except for Christopher who was positive with a spot on his lung!

At the hospital when the doctor told me that my six year old had TB, I lost it and had trouble controlling my tears. When the doctor was finally able to speak to me, he said Christopher would have to be admitted to hospital for treatment. To me it was a death knell as I had known the danger of TB in my youth where children and teenagers died. I was terrified.

After a few days, the doctor admitted Ted, Chris' younger brother, to keep him company even though Ted was TB negative. I'm not sure it worked out well as reports were that Chris and Ted at five and six years fought and chased each other around, much to the chagrin of the staff and probably the patients too!

We lived about fifteen minutes from the hospital and for the first week or so I was able to keep up the nightly routine of bathing them until I was stopped because it was after hours! From then on I visited daily and gave support to Christopher who had to endure daily stomach washings via a tube passed through his nose. His memory of that time is one of a very long, lonely time. After a month the boys were discharged and much to everyone's joy, we were a family again. After a year on medications especially developed for TB, Chris was deemed "cured" although he still carries a scar on his lung that could become active if his health deteriorates.

When we moved to Ottawa, we brought the contents of our small bungalow in Don Mills and had not added much furniture as we couldn't afford it after buying the Stibbard house. Now, I needed to find pieces that didn't cost too much to flesh out the pieces we had to furnish this big farmhouse. I took to going to country auctions to augment what we had brought from Toronto. It was a great time to collect, as many of the old family farms close to Ottawa were closing down. Soon I had all we needed but it was too much fun to stop, so I opened a Canadiana store in my summer kitchen.

Summer kitchens were an addition to the main house in the old days of wood stoves and were used for cooking there in the hottest months, thus moving the heat from the main kitchen. In our house, a door out of the kitchen led into a three-story addition complete with a walk-in basement. I cleaned up furniture and stripped and refinished many pieces. Business was OK, and when we were moved back to Toronto two years later we brought back the leftovers from the auction we held to get rid of much of my stock.

On our return to Toronto, having had my appetite whetted in Ottawa for Canadian history, I joined the North York Historical Society. The Society's project at that time was the restoration of Gibson House in North York, just up Toronto's Yonge St. It was the home of David Gibson who was an ally of William Lyon Mackenzie in the rebellion of 1837. After it was open to the public awhile I felt it needed someone to tell visitors its story. The society agreed, and I was happy to form a group of volunteers and help train them. We were given many lectures and workshops on the earlier ways of life and our volunteer group was known in our field for its professionalism.

After a couple of years, I was offered a job with the Ontario Historical Society to research and provide guidelines for restoring and furnishing the Ball House in Ball's Falls on the Niagara Peninsula. It was very satisfying taking off the layers of wallpaper and paint to get down to the earlier period. When I was offered the opportunity to do the same for the home of the Canadian World War I ace Billy Bishop in Owen Sound—some three hours' drive from Toronto—I declined. I'd had enough of travelling back and forth, and that was the end of my historical restoration work.

In the meantime, we were involved in the restoration of our own early Canadian log house just north of Minden, Ontario, which we bought from Len's Aunt Winnie after Uncle Wesley died. It needed a lot of work. It was a shabby clapboarded settler's first log house built to the minimum requirements for obtaining a grant from the Crown in 1866. To get his land the settler had to build a house not less than sixteen by twenty feet, usually of logs from the property. He also had to clear four acres, build a barn and keep up the road in front. All within four years.

For people mostly from the British Isles, it was a chance to own land, which was impossible for them at home.

Our place was on Bobcaygeon Road six kilometers north of Minden in Haliburton county. This road was built by the government in the 1880s to connect with a road from Lake Ontario and bring large groups of newcomers to this still virgin land. They had answered the government's call for men to log its vast forests, which supplied the British Navy with tall masts and furniture makers in England with pine. The descendants, many from Ireland, are still there.

We called it the "farm" because Len's Uncle Wesley had started to turn it into a Christmas tree farm and had planted many pines before dying suddenly of a heart attack. We furnished the house with items from about the mid- to late-1800s. Many were pieces from the Ottawa store. We enjoyed this retreat for forty years until both of us no longer had the energy to run it—especially chopping and bringing in the wood we needed for the fireplace and our wonderful Finlay Oval wood-stove in the kitchen. That stove had a warming oven across the top and I really loved it! In our first twenty years before electricity came up the road, the stove also heated our entire three-bedroom log house.

We mostly went to the "farm" in the fall, winter and spring. Our winter routine when the boys were young was to leave the car at the foot of our hill and each person carried a box of supplies through hip-deep snow stepping each time in a new spot. By the third and last trip they would be walking on a hard packed path—hard work! After the first trip, Mother would stay in the house, light the Coleman oil lamps and get the big wood-stove going. By the time someone had gone to the well, broken the ice and brought back the two buckets of water, the big kitchen was fairly warm and we each soon had a steaming mug of cocoa.

Sometimes if it weren't too late, I would mix a batch of bread, pack it away on the couch under lots of coats and in the morning would cut off pieces of the risen dough and fry them in the big iron frying pan. In Newfoundland these were called "toutons" and were eaten with butter and sweet molasses. Later, some of the dough would appear as sticky "Chelsea buns" and loaves of bread baked in the wood-stove in iron bread pans, which held the heat as the temperature fluctuated with the fire!

We all enjoyed the change of surroundings, even Len, when, on his first winter trip, realized that he wouldn't freeze to death! We took a brick to bed that had been heated in the oven and wrapped in a sock. Our beds were further warmed by "eiderdowns" given by several of our friends who donated down "eiderdowns," a part of their mother's "hope chest" in the twenties.

I felt it important that our city-bred sons be taught that they didn't need all the city amenities to survive and thrive. This basic living taught them resilience, too, and they soon wanted to bring friends to show them a new way of living without electricity or plumbing! Even though we were within 120 miles of Toronto and only six from town, electricity and telephone did not reach us for twenty more years! As for me, it was a return to the environment of my youth, and I loved every minute of it.

After forty years there we sold it when Len and I found it was too much for us. Our sons, though they loved it, knew that it wouldn't work for their families, so we had no choice. A sad day but necessary. Occasionally now I rent it for Easter or Thanksgiving, and we have a family time there enjoying the lovely place that gave us such precious memories. The current owners have become friends and have been generous in taking me up there for a few days now and then.

We have also been able to give Ted a trip there occasionally. He has a close connection with the old place as he and Beverley lived there with their three-month-old daughter, Alexa, for a year and a half when it had no electricity, bathroom, running water or central heat! He loves it. To do this, Chris rents a large vehicle with accommodation for Ted's large wheelchair and his Hoyer lift. Ted's caregiver, Tracey, brings all the equipment and supplies for his total care and together they share his night-time turning. It's a real expedition, but it gives Ted a most welcome change from his apartment. The scenery and country air is a treat for everybody.

When the boys were young, most summers centred around a wilderness canoe trip usually to Lake Temagami, a huge, beautiful, sparsely-populated lake in indigenous country four hours north of Toronto. Lake Temagami held many happy memories for Len. As a child in the 1930s when his father had a part interest in Temagami Lodge, Torontonians and some Americans would come there for a northern experience that included fishing and shore dinners. They took a train and finally a boat to this north country paradise. Len's family used to leave the day school closed and come back in time for school opening in September. It was heaven for a nine-year-old, and our sons grew to love it too. As an adult, Christopher has taken his son, Ben, camping on this beloved lake as well as doing a couple of solo trips.

To get to Temagami we drove around four and a half hours north to an access road to the lake. Before long we would be on the lake looking for a campsite to put up tents for the night. One year we took a dog and two cats, one of whom was very pregnant. The cats were understandably terrified. Once on the lake with the shore vanishing, one scared cat tried to jump to dry land. She didn't make it. The bedraggled cat soon settled down to lick herself dry in the bottom of the canoe.

Most days we paddled all day with stops for swimming and picnics and sometimes to portage into an inner lake. Portaging meant unloading everything and carrying it overland to the next body of water. These paths through the woods were sometimes so worn down as to be almost ditches having been used by moccasined feet for thousands of years.

A big part of this adventure was not having any plans beyond where we were eventually heading. We left our watches in the car and broke camp after breakfast each day hoping for no rain! There were lots of islands for swimming and shore lunches with a fire for boiling the blackened triangular tea kettle (from Newfoundland) for a "mug-up." It also served as rest stops for the adults! We hoped to find an unoccupied site before too far and before dark.

If it were raining, "mug-ups" were especially welcome. We would head for a forested shore where we would start a fire even in a downpour! The boys knew where to find dry tinder next to the trunks of the pine trees and once we had spread our raincoats above the struggling little fire and it caught, we could add dry branches. A cup of tea as we waited out the storm was a welcome respite!

The Ojibway people who lived on Bear Island, which was their reservation, were very friendly and ran the Hudson's Bay Store there. We always made a stop there for a treat of ice cream! Bear Island was where the young Englishman Archie Belaney learned to be indigenous and took the name of Gray Owl, Canada's first conservationist.

We usually set up our tents on an island—safer from bears—and wolfed down a pot of whatever dried food emerged from our kitchen bag. If we had been lucky and found berries, I would make berry dumplings—a big hit! On the last night out, I would combine the leftover peanut butter, dried milk, raisins and honey and call it halva. It was popular too!

Before leaving home we would have had a supplies packing night when we made our bannock mix. On the trip it needed only water to make pancake batter or a biscuit-like dough, which we fried to make bannock. We found a way to do it even in the rain!

Years later in our late fifties with our sons now tripping on their own and our not having done any tripping for years, Len and I had a yen to return to Lake Temagami! We thought there must be others who had been trippers in their youth and who, in their late middle age, thought they were now too old! So, we advertised in a small publication geared to living fully and soon we had four adventurers willing to trust us! No fee was involved other than sharing the costs, and we set out with these older adventurers.

At the beginning, midway and our last night out we held sharing sessions, which were useful as we processed what we had been experiencing. We had learned that we had unknown inner resources, and all agreed it had been a great adventure. We repeated it for several more years.

RETIREMENT

Len retired at fifty-five when big changes happened at IBM. It was the year when personal computers became popular and began to be sold in stores. IBM no longer needed salesmen to call on companies to sell office products.

When Len retired and we had this new-found "freedom" we decided to rent our Toronto house and live in another country for a year. Our children were now on their own and there was nothing to hold us back. A couple of days later I mentioned this idea to a friend. She called the next day to say there was a notice on the Faculty Club board at the University of Toronto of a flat to rent in Kensington, London. A few months later in September, 1980, we were in England.

On our first Wednesday there we went to Northumbria House just off Trafalgar Square for their Commonwealth coffee hour where we met people from all over the Commonwealth. We were approached by a woman who asked if we would like to be volunteers at Westminster Abbey! Would we!! So, for the month of November, we were given a tea at five o'clock in the Jerusalem Chamber off the main body of the abbey and sent to different spots in the abbey to make sure nobody left unattended parcels. London had had several bombing incidents but there were none in the abbey—thank goodness—and we got to know the abbey fairly well as we were stationed in pairs so we could take turns walking around with our guidebooks.

It was a wonderful year filled with touring and doing all the things that one couldn't do on a three week holiday!

Our Westminster friend, Bertha Barnardiston, published a sheet called *Welcome to Westminster* that listed many activities and events in the Westminster district and in London generally that were free. Len helped her produce it. If the event wasn't free she seemed to know who had free tickets—the Chelsea Flower Show and Wimbledon for instance, which Len and I took advantage of! At some events, people would present their admission tickets and on getting them passed back would then pass them on to someone else! I have a feeling the practice was no secret to the event sponsors!

Britain was celebrating the influence of French architecture after the Norman Conquest and Bertha invited us to a meeting of the British Architectural Society. The Society was organizing a trip to Normandy to look at original architecture that had found its way to Britain. We eagerly signed up. Normandy was beautiful in the spring with irises blooming along the ridge pole of slanted roofs. The trip included a visit to Claude Monet's famous "Giverny" where he painted his bridge and water lily pond. Such a treat!

OTHER WANDERINGS

Once, our Toronto friends, Em and Brian MacConnell who lived in London, lent us their car and we drove to Wales to visit Dylan Thomas' home, Brown's Hotel and his burial place in Larghan. We bought *A Child's Christmas in Wales* there, which we read every Christmas.

We also had friends in Brussels, Pam and Ken Ducommun. Ken and Len had been friends in Vancouver and the Ducommuns invited us for Christmas. It was very special to be with them and we were included in invitations to their friends' open houses. Although our French was pretty rudimentary, we managed and thoroughly enjoyed ourselves.

Later that year the Ducommuns invited us to share their Riviera rental on the Cote d' Azure in August when most people go on holidays. Ted, who had recently come to England to work, came with us. The gorgeous beaches of the Mediterranean and the motor trips inland to the lavender fields made for great memories! I have a picture of Ted walking "Pont du Gard," a three-level structure built by the Romans spanning a very deep gorge. He was the only one of us brave enough to do it!

On our way back through France we decided to detour to visit the grave of my mother's brother, Uncle Will Norman, who was killed in WW1. As we got closer, following small country roads, I realized that I had no flowers to take to the grave and asked Len to stop at a house that had turned its living room into a small store. He couldn't stop there but stopped at a second house that also had a little store. As I began to gather some artificial flowers, I became aware that the proprietress was watching me intently. I told her in my halting French that my uncle was buried in the cemetery down the road. At that she began to tell me an unbelievable story.

During WW1, her aunt's small farm was close to the front lines and had been chosen by the Allies as a site to establish a rest area for troops who were pulled back from the front lines every couple of weeks. One day a group of soldiers were practicing grenade throwing and when it was Uncle Will's turn the grenade went off prematurely in his hand! Her aunt brought out her own sheets to wrap the body pieces and helped to bury Uncle Will in the nearby cemetery. From that day forward, her aunt looked after Uncle Will's grave as though it were that of her own son who was missing in action. As a child, the lady to whom I was speaking had helped her aunt. After her aunt's death she continued to look after Uncle Will's grave.

What were the chances of our stopping at the right house?

We came home from England in early September. Shortly after returning home we were approached by Kingview to have a Toronto centre in our home. We'd had an earlier connection with Kingview, a spiritual community on the outskirts of Toronto that was based on the idea of living life with integrity and spontaneity. This approach to living, along with its lectures, appealed to us so we said "yes."

So, for almost seven years we lived as a community in our Stibbard Ave. house. Sometimes there were six or seven of us including two-year-old twins! It was an enriching time in our lives. One winter while living in community, Len and I decided to spend a month at a community in South Africa, a short distance from Cape Town in the Stellenbosch wine growing region. It was beautiful fertile countryside and the community was living in a Dutch style house whose date of 1778 was over the front door! These homes resembled the style of the conquerors' homes back in Holland.

The road up the coast to Durban was gorgeous, overlooking both mountains and sea. I have never been in a more beautiful country. While there we were taken north to KwaZulu to meet Grace and Absalom Makatini, a Zulu couple who lived in a tiny village and who led a small group that were teaching an approach to living life in positive ways. We were put up in a typical round Zulu dwelling with a conical roof—very comfortable. Grace tried to teach me how to carry a large pail of water from the river on my head as she did so easily. No success!

More than a century before, the Zulu people were known as fearsome warriors as they fought to preserve their land from the encroachment of Europeans. Zululand, as it was known then, has its own king and is a semi-autonomous part of South Africa now called KwaZulu.

NEW HORIZONS

While living in community, I was still very connected to my old friends in Toronto, many of whom were dealing with issues such as empty nest, menopause, health problems and ageing. So, in January '87 three of us met around my dining room table to discuss an idea that had been growing for some time. We felt it was time to find new ways of dealing with our common issues and of working together rather than struggling in isolation. Problems give us an opportunity to learn life's lessons, and it looked as if we would have lots of material for learning and finding new meaning!

Many women joined us over the thirty years that we met. We learned from each other and we used different books' themes as springboards for discussions related to our own living. We grew old together—hopefully older and wiser!

About this time, I became aware of the American Holistic Nurses' Association (AHNA), which resurrected my old interest in healing. Their approach was one of recognizing that human beings share a connection to the universal energy that animates all living things. The Association taught us a way of connecting to this balanced state both for oneself and the individual one is working with. This practice made a lot of sense to me, so I added the training to my arsenal of helpful approaches to health.

A teacher of this work from England, Gemma Walker, who was lecturing in Canada and the United States at this time, joined us for one of our meetings. She taught us how to mend strained relationships by repeatedly sending love to the situation during meditation. Several of us can attest to its effectiveness!

Gemma and I became friends and twice, once with Len, I participated in her yearly retreat on the island of Iona in Scotland where people came together to relax, meditate and fill themselves with the atmosphere of this special Isle. Its importance springs from St. Columba who left Ireland and established a monastery there bringing Christianity to Europe in the sixth century.

At Toronto's cancer centre, Princess Margaret Hospital, they were offering a programme that resonated with my own work, and I became a volunteer there. This programme, developed by Dr. Alastair Cunningham, a psychologist, taught people a way to use their minds to reduce mental suffering and promote healing of their body, in addition to medical treatment. It was available to anyone who came to the hospital as patient or support person. Published research on the programme showed that when people with terminal diagnoses became very involved with this kind of self-healing, they often lived much longer than their doctors predicted. The programme also introduced members to the basic ideas and techniques of spiritual growth, which reveals that there is much more to oneself than body and mind. I volunteered there every week for twenty years and found it valuable for my own outlook on life.

Eventually, because Ted and his little family were coming to live with us for a while, the community found another location and it was a Tyrrell home once again.

While in England we had become friends with Anne-Marie Fyne who contacted us a few months after our return about her protege, Stephen Hemstead. His gap year was coming up and he was interested in gaining experience in fish culture before starting university the next year. We found him a placement in Nova Scotia, with our home being his home away from home. His grateful parents invited us to visit them in Kenya. After several nudges we decided to go and flew to Nairobi.

The Hemsteads had a flower farm in the Rift Valley and exported agapanthus (Bare Naked Ladies) to Europe. It was almost at the equator but because it was at an elevation, we were most comfortable. Because of the abysmal conditions of the Kenyan roads, most farmers, including our friend, owned a small plane for business. We were on the receiving end of several flights, one of which took us over Victoria Falls and then on to a resort on Lake Victoria. What an experience to see these fabled sights!

A few days later, Edmund, our friend, flew us to Governor's Camp, a safari establishment in Masai country where we observed lions, cheetahs, elephants, giraffes and other animals on short trips in the countryside. The camp had no fences and left no garbage so as to leave as little impact on the earth as possible. We were told the land we were on belonged to the animals and as we were on their territory they had rights as well. There was usually a small herd of elephants at the entrance. One thing I found fascinating was that the nursing mother's breasts were forward at a spot corresponding to a human's and not back toward the hind end as all other female animals' were. Also, they did not have udders but just two breasts shaped like a human's!

We were warned not to leave our tents at night but to signal with our flashlights for the night watchmen who watched for animals at night! One morning we found the grass around our tent was closely mowed next to our sleeping heads! It was explained as a nightly activity of the hippo who live just down the bank.

The Masai, who still live in their round enclosures with their cattle in a separate one next to theirs, love their cattle. The cattle provide a lot of their diet, which is a mixture of milk and blood obtained by puncturing a neck vein. Everybody looked healthy.

We learned that a young man could not marry until he killed his first lion with nothing but two sticks. When thrown at the lion, the short stick stuns him and the longer one then can be used to dispatch him. The young man is then entitled to wear a red blanket over his shoulder. Very impressive.

We didn't learn whether the young Masai men employed at the camp were entitled to their own blankets!

The annual migration of wildebeest back to the south across the Mara River started the next day, and these animals gathered at the river's edge all day and night. Before long there were thousands pushing the front line who hesitated because of the crocodiles waiting in the shallow water. I saw only one get caught by the crocodile, which, satisfied, left the others to swim to safety and continue their journey.

WALKING THE CAMINO

One day Len came home and announced he and a friend were going to walk across Spain. I wasn't greatly surprised but thought they were crazy! They persuaded me to attend a lecture by a local Anglican minister who had just walked the Camino de Santiago. It sounded interesting but was not for me!

Within a few days Len's friend announced that he couldn't go as his wife refused to give him the money, so Len now had to find another partner—me. He persuaded me to attend a lunch with two other interested people, one of whom was from Spain. She assured me that if I found I couldn't continue on the trip, there was a country bus available.

So, I, who had walked only six kilometers once in my life, found myself getting into shape by walking from our home near Lawrence Ave. down Yonge St. to King St. where we bought equipment. Then we walked back home again with twenty pounds of cans in our backpacks! It was a distance of about six miles at least!

The Camino de Santiago is an ancient pilgrimage route for Christians who could no longer make the pilgrimage to Jerusalem at the time of the Crusades. These days, people walk from Italy, Holland, France and Spain to walk the Camino!

We started in France at the little village of St. Jean de Pied au Port at the foot of the Napoleonic Pass. It seemed anything but a pass to me as we climbed a twenty-degree grade all day! By the time we reached Roncesvalles and the monastery on the Spanish side, I fell into bed with my boots on after walking twenty-four kilometers on our first day—half of it was uphill! Later that evening, Len and I attended the special mass in their chapel for blessing the peregrinos (pilgrims) before their long walk. We felt we could use it!

We walked every day except two, and before long the exhilaration of eighteen to twenty kilometers a day felt natural though exhausting! Only once did we have to backtrack when we missed the small daub of yellow paint that indicated the correct route. It was on the plain outside Pamplona.

Everyone walked at their own pace and we usually met up with others at the refugio at the end of the day to exchange stories. But first we took a shower (warm if we were early enough) and washed shirts and socks. The air was so dry the laundry was always dry before we went to bed!

We met many people from all over the world. We discovered that one white-haired couple whom we frequently saw at the end of the day and referred to as the "old couple" were younger than we were!

The Basque people on whose land we were travelling in the north of Spain were lovely to us—sometimes a meal, a swig from a wineskin or directions. All roadside signs were in Basque and Spanish as they yearned to be independent.

On a ridge of hills that ended the Pamplona Plain, we could see for miles. A small village below looked like heaven to me. I told Len that that village was as far as my weary body could take me and that was where I was going to sleep that night no matter what! We descended the steep hill and found ourselves in a village that was deserted except for a couple of young girls pushing a baby carriage. We were in the middle of making eating signs when a woman in a car stopped. She spoke no English but motioned us to get in, drove us to her home, gave us drinks on her patio, cooked us a meal for which she refused payment and drove us to an almost finished refugio. Such hospitality!

When we reached Santiago de Compostela, we went straight to the cathedral where the relics (bones) of St. James are held and performed the ritual of placing our hands on his statue. This place has become so indented by hundreds of years of hands as to be at least an inch deep! We visited the church office where we presented our "passport," which we had had stamped at the end of each day. After confirming that we had indeed walked the whole route, we were given our certificate.

Later that day we attended a mass in the cathedral where our names were read out along with the others who had arrived that day. We were awestruck by the giant censor hanging from the high ceiling that left giant puffs of smoke as it swung in a giant arc. Memorable.

We arrived home on Len's Birthday to a big birthday party. He was seventy and I sixty-eight, and we had just walked 900 kilometres in seven weeks. I wouldn't have missed it for anything, but once was enough! I had only ridden the bus two days when I had had an inflamed fibula, common to many "peregrinos."

FIFTY YEARS TOGETHER

Our fiftieth anniversary was coming up in 2002, and to mark it we decided to see the Arctic. It had always held a fascination for us and when we read the ad for Adventure Canada's trip there—small ship, small number of passengers, historical sites, lecturers on board who would later lead related shore expeditions—we were excited.

The coast of Greenland came first. We stopped in various places of interest including Disco Bay where the glacier was calving off huge icebergs that eventually find their way to Newfoundland. We crossed Davis Strait to Canada and put in at several Inuit communities where we were treated to amazing displays of balance and strength and in some were offered opportunities to buy their famous carvings. Everyone was friendly and we were impressed at the way babies and small children snuggled in their mother's large hoods—"amautis." This company left a gift of money at each stop in appreciation of their hospitality.

The ship carried experts who lectured on their specialty before leading groups ashore to examine archeological sites. Our ship followed Lancaster Sound to the famed Northwest Passage, and we were taken ashore at Beechey Island where Sir John Franklin and his two icebound ships spent two winters. Four of Franklin's crew are buried there. Strewn around the graves are the tin cans with their lumps of lead solder, which didn't help their health! It's awe-inspiring to realize everything was as it was left over 140 years before.

Other experts giving lectures on board included Margaret Atwood who spoke on the art—and work—of writing!

To see this part of our country that was above the Arctic Circle was more than we expected. Its vastness covered by so much ice was mind-boggling as were the amazing people who have carved out a way of life that has sustained them for thousands of years.

What an incredible country Canada is.

CHANGES

After another decade when we had reached our eighties, we found that keeping up a big house began to be too much to manage. Len was finding it harder to do his part of the upkeep and more and more of it fell to me. To make our income go farther, we had been renting our downstairs apartment. Among other things, being a landlady demanded more energy than I had, so we decided to move to a retirement residence. Len was very loathe to leave the house where five generations of Tyrrell voices had been heard, but we didn't have much choice.

We moved to Christie Gardens, an established retirement residence in midtown Toronto and bought a two-bedroom Life Lease apartment with a very large terrace that had been planted by the former owner. There were trees, shrubs and flower beds so it was like having a backyard again with our new lawn furniture. We enjoyed it and soon Len was saying, "This was the smartest thing we could have done!"

We chose this as our new home because, besides having an all-round stimulating environment, it also had a care facility for those who needed more care than could be provided at home. As Len's slight dementia increased, looking after him became increasingly difficult to the point it was affecting my own health, so I followed the doctor's advice to admit him to the care floor.

As he became more disoriented at home, I had been helping him make sense of the things that were confusing him, but this was becoming more and more difficult as his condition worsened. Occasionally though, his thinking cleared somewhat, and he was aware of how difficult it was for both of us. One day he said to me, "If this is too much for you, I'm willing to give you a divorce,"—what love!

Moving him and separating us after sixty years of marriage was the hardest thing I have ever had to do. It felt like I was abandoning him at a time when he needed me most. We had always been each other's closest confidants. Gradually he became less worried as he gave up trying to figure out things. Because he wasn't at some distant nursing home but was just down a short trip on an elevator, we were able to spend quality time together attending special events, barbecues, sing-alongs (which he enjoyed) and especially time in the courtyard garden in the summer. We frequently had family gatherings in my apartment, too, which he enjoyed.

In his fourth year in care, he became much weaker. He spent most of his time sleeping in his wheelchair and became weaker and weaker. A few days before he died, he said to me "Thank you for loving me." I wept.

Shortly afterwards Len's doctor discovered his breathing had deteriorated into what he recognized as a final stage. Len stayed in bed that day and when he took his final breath at 12:04 a.m. on December 30, 2017, Paul, Christopher, grandson Ben and I were with him. As hearing is the last sense to go, we told him to go when he was ready, that we would be all right as we had each other. Such a final moment!

I was sad but relieved at the same time. Len had put in some long, hard years and I couldn't wish him back no matter how much I missed him. I was now alone after sixty-five years with him. I felt numb though relieved that his long ordeal was over. He had given me a wonderful life and had worked hard to provide for us. We were comfortable though we had to watch our spending, had wonderful trips both with IBM and on our own, and cherished our time with our family at the "farm," on canoe and car trips.

After Len's death, I moved through the necessaries in a fog as Paul and Chris took over and did what had to be done. They were wonderful and were such a blessing to me. We had a private family funeral on the third day and laid him to rest with David in the family plot in Mt. Pleasant cemetery as he had requested. It was a hard day for all of us.

Life goes on. Five weeks later brought another milestone. I had been feeling unwell for some time with indigestion and general tiredness but put it down to being ninety years old—what did I expect!! However, one night I began to feel worse than usual with vomiting and diarrhea. Because I was losing so much fluid I felt I should go to the hospital where I would get the fluids replaced, so off I went in an ambulance ordered by our night nurse.

Bright and early the next morning I was taken for a CAT scan that revealed I had a mass (later reported to be cancer) in my ascending colon. Not being fond of fixing every last thing by the latest intervention, I decided at almost ninety-one to do nothing and live out my remaining time thinking of it in terms of years. When a palliative care doctor told me my time was measured in weeks, not years, it didn't take me long to change my mind and say "yes" to the surgery. I still had a lot of living to do!

A year and a half later the tests show an "all clear." As it was stage three cancer, I'll continue to be checked for two years. Two and a half hours of anaesthetic didn't do anything for my brain either, but my memory loss is minimal—I think!

At any rate, I'm enjoying finishing up this story in January of 2020!

REFLECTIONS

As I reflect on the events of my long life and the events that shaped me there are a few that stand out:

The death of both my parents by the time I was fifteen made me resilient. I had to leave two homes and cultures, each time leaving behind a parent, friends and a way of life that was all I had ever known. I knew there was nothing that could be done about it, so I buried my feelings.

As I grew to realize that I was only one of the many who was finding life hard I developed a way of looking at things: it was not "why me?" but "why not me?"

It helped me remember that one just gets on with difficult things. It was something I had learned as a child. Doing that opens one up to seeing the things that are working out, and one's view of life becomes more balanced. At least that's the outlook that worked for me.

At my uncle's home nobody mentioned my family or the events that had brought me there, and I felt a bit like a nobody. At home in St. George's and Clarke's Beach, I had been an important part of the family, but not here. I couldn't help with anything—the cooking, the dishes or the lunches. Not only that, my uncle took it upon himself to cure me of my Newfoundland accent and that only added to the feeling that I was a lesser person than I had been in my family home. I had been brought up mostly on the west coast of Newfoundland where the accent of Devon and Dorset didn't exist as it did in the earlier settled villages of Newfoundland's east coast. In Newfoundland my accent was considered more Canadian! After I had spent three years at Oakwood Collegiate I sounded like a Torontonian—I just hadn't been aware of the change!

Looking back, I wish I had been more affectionate with my children, but I wasn't aware that there was a lack. My own upbringing didn't include affection though there was no doubt of my parents' love. So that expression of affection was missing in me and now, remembering those days, I'm sorry for it. Affection is something that is reassuring for anyone, especially children.

During my training at Wellesley Hospital, I met people, including patients, to whom I could relate and made friends with some. Those were people who felt more like the family I remembered and whose interests and values were similar to mine. I felt I had made the right decision to become a nurse and could move easily in that circle. My new confidence didn't mean that I turned my back on the people who had helped me—only on my uncle's values, which were mostly negative. It was good to have moved away from that.

When I met Len in Vancouver, I felt that he was a perfect fit to my approach to life though perhaps a bit more hesitant. His values and mine clicked and we learned from each other. We made a good team!

Though I am now on my own, I have three sons whom I love and who love me. We share a special bond. I am blessed.

Living in a vibrant retirement community, I know I made the right decision twelve years ago. I have found stimulation in the many opportunities provided here as well as in the many new friends I have made. I'm glad that when circumstances pointed toward that big decision for us, we did it before we absolutely had to. It gave us a chance to establish ourselves in our new setting and begin the next phase of our lives.

When I begin to miss the physical prowess that I once had, I remind myself of Keats' poem:

An aged man is but a paltry thing,
A tattered cloak upon a stick, unless
Soul clap its hands and sing, and louder sing
For every tatter in its mortal dress.

I know that I have a limited time left, and I am OK with that. I have had a life filled with adventure. I learned early that one can't hang on to life as it is because it often presents other plans. I hope I've learned to say "yes" to life. There may be lots of adventures out there waiting for me!

And the greatest adventure of all could be just around the corner waiting for this ninety-three-year-old!

POSTSCRIPT

It's now 2019 as I'm finishing this three-part story. The 140-year-old house in St. George's is still a family home. It still sits there with its front door looking out to sea although half the grassy field has been taken over by blueberry bushes. The house is now owned by a local family who have lovingly retained the original clapboard after installing exterior insulation. Much of the interior still has the flavour of the 1800s.

The house is the only original one remaining on the bank, the others having fallen victim to 140 years of weathering and deterioration. The bank road, which was used as much as the newer High Road when I was a child, is now only useable in parts. Much of it has succumbed to erosion. The part opposite the house is still useable for a few hundred yards. The beach below is somewhat narrower but is still guarded by the same red sandstone cliffs that gave Phyllis and me the potting clay we fashioned into marbles and saucers. Some things haven't changed!

Sandy Point across the harbour is deserted. The exodus from Sandy Point that started when the railway came through in the late 1800s was completed when the remaining few families were moved under the government's resettlement plan in the 1960s. Children play and swim at Red Rocks still and all summer the wind blows steadily from the Gulf of St. Lawrence. And the sunsets are still unbelievably gorgeous!

When Phyllis died of a heart attack in her home in California in 1996, we honoured her request that her ashes be scattered in the sea in front of the house where she was born. When my time comes, half my ashes will join Len's and David's in Toronto, and half will join hers in our original home in Newfoundland.

CPSIA information can be obtained
at www.ICGtesting.com
Printed in the USA
BVHW070100120920
588315BV00002B/10

9 780228 823162